Confucianism: A Very Short Introduction

VERY SHORT INTRODUCTIONS are for anyone wanting a stimulating and accessible way in to a new subject. They are written by experts and have been translated into more than 40 different languages.

The series began in 1995 and now covers a wide variety of topics in every discipline. The VSI library now contains nearly 400 volumes—a Very Short Introduction to everything from Indian philosophy to psychology and American History—and continues to grow in every subject area.

Very Short Introductions available now:

ACCOUNTING Christopher Nobes
ADVERTISING Winston Fletcher
AFRICAN HISTORY John Parker and
    Richard Rathbone
AFRICAN RELIGIONS
    Jacob K. Olupona
AGNOSTICISM Robin Le Poidevin
ALEXANDER THE GREAT
    Hugh Bowden
AMERICAN HISTORY Paul S. Boyer
AMERICAN IMMIGRATION
    David A. Gerber
AMERICAN LEGAL HISTORY
    G. Edward White
AMERICAN POLITICAL PARTIES
    AND ELECTIONS L. Sandy Maisel
AMERICAN POLITICS Richard M. Valelly
THE AMERICAN PRESIDENCY
    Charles O. Jones
ANAESTHESIA Aidan O'Donnell
ANARCHISM Colin Ward
ANCIENT EGYPT Ian Shaw
ANCIENT GREECE Paul Cartledge
THE ANCIENT NEAR EAST
    Amanda H. Podany
ANCIENT PHILOSOPHY Julia Annas
ANCIENT WARFARE Harry Sidebottom
ANGELS David Albert Jones
ANGLICANISM Mark Chapman
THE ANGLO-SAXON AGE John Blair
THE ANIMAL KINGDOM
    Peter Holland
ANIMAL RIGHTS David DeGrazia
THE ANTARCTIC Klaus Dodds
ANTISEMITISM Steven Beller

ANXIETY Daniel Freeman and
    Jason Freeman
THE APOCRYPHAL GOSPELS
    Paul Foster
ARCHAEOLOGY Paul Bahn
ARCHITECTURE Andrew Ballantyne
ARISTOCRACY William Doyle
ARISTOTLE Jonathan Barnes
ART HISTORY Dana Arnold
ART THEORY Cynthia Freeland
ASTROBIOLOGY David C. Catling
ATHEISM Julian Baggini
AUGUSTINE Henry Chadwick
AUSTRALIA Kenneth Morgan
AUTISM Uta Frith
THE AVANT GARDE
    David Cottington
THE AZTECS David Carrasco
BACTERIA Sebastian G. B. Amyes
BARTHES Jonathan Culler
THE BEATS David Sterritt
BEAUTY Roger Scruton
BESTSELLERS John Sutherland
THE BIBLE John Riches
BIBLICAL ARCHAEOLOGY
    Eric H. Cline
BIOGRAPHY Hermione Lee
THE BLUES Elijah Wald
THE BOOK OF MORMON
    Terryl Givens
BORDERS Alexander C. Diener and
    Joshua Hagen
THE BRAIN Michael O'Shea
THE BRITISH CONSTITUTION
    Martin Loughlin

Daniel K. Gardner

CONFUCIANISM

A Very Short Introduction

OXFORD
UNIVERSITY PRESS

OXFORD
UNIVERSITY PRESS

Oxford University Press is a department of the
University of Oxford. It furthers the University's objective
of excellence in research, scholarship, and education
by publishing worldwide.

Oxford   New York
Auckland   Cape Town   Dar es Salaam   Hong Kong   Karachi
Kuala Lumpur   Madrid   Melbourne   Mexico City   Nairobi
New Delhi   Shanghai   Taipei   Toronto

With offices in
Argentina   Austria   Brazil   Chile   Czech Republic   France   Greece
Guatemala   Hungary   Italy   Japan   Poland   Portugal   Singapore
South Korea   Switzerland   Thailand   Turkey   Ukraine   Vietnam

Oxford is a registered trade mark of Oxford University Press
in the UK and certain other countries.

Published in the United States of America by
Oxford University Press
198 Madison Avenue, New York, NY 10016

Library of Congress Cataloging-in-Publication Data
Gardner, Daniel K., 1950- author.
Confucianism / Daniel K. Gardner.
pages   cm—(A very short introduction)
Includes bibliographical references and index.
ISBN 978-0-19-539891-5 (paperback)
1. Confucianism.   I. Title.
BL1853.G37   2014
181'.112—dc23   2014021169

Printed by Integrated Books International, United States of America
on acid-free paper

Acknowledgments

My sincerest thanks go to Cynthia Brokaw of Brown University. She listened attentively to my ideas, read drafts of chapters, and urged me forward when I was dragging. Every writer should be so fortunate to have a colleague—and friend—like her.

Cynthia Read, my editor at Oxford University Press, and her assistant, Charlotte Steinhardt, were unfailingly supportive of this project from the start. Anonymous readers for the Press provided especially thoughtful and thorough reviews of the manuscript. This book owes much to their professional generosity. Kristina Johnson assisted in the final stages of the editing process. I am thankful for her sharp set of eyes and sound judgment.

Contents

List of illustrations

Chronology

Shang Dynasty, ca. 1600 BCE–ca. 1045 BCE
Zhou Dynasty, ca. 1045 BCE–ca. 256 BCE
    Western Zhou, ca. 1046 BCE–771 BCE
        King Wen (11th c. BCE)
        King Wu (11th c. BCE)
        Duke of Zhou (11th c. BCE)
    Eastern Zhou, 771 BCE–256 BCE
        Spring and Autumn Period, 722–481 BCE
        Confucius (551 BCE–479 BCE)
        Warring States Period, 403 BCE–221 BCE
        Mencius (4th c. BCE)
        Xunzi (3rd c. BCE)
Qin Dynasty, 221 BCE–206 BCE
Han Dynasty, 206 BCE–220 CE
    Western Han, 206 BCE–9 CE
        Confucianism established as state teaching under Emperor Wu
        (r. 141 BCE–87 BCE)
    Wang Mang interregnum, 9–23
    Eastern Han, 25–220
Six Dynasties, 220–589
Sui Dynasty, 581–618
    Civil service examinations implemented countrywide
Tang Dynasty, 618–907
Five Dynasties, 907–60
Song Dynasty, 960–1279
    Northern Song, 960–1127

Major Neo-Confucian thinkers:
    Zhou Dunyi (1017–73)
    Zhang Zai (1020–77)
    Cheng Hao (1032–85)
    Cheng Yi (1033–1107)
Southern Song, 1127–1279
    Neo-Confucian synthesis:
    Zhu Xi (1130–1200)
Yuan Dynasty, 1279–1368
Ming Dynasty, 1368–1644
    Wang Yangming (1472–1522) School of Neo-Confucianism
Qing Dynasty, 1644–1912
    Civil service examinations system abolished (1905)
Republic, 1912–49
    May Fourth Movement (protests begin on May 4, 1919)
    Chiang Kai-shek (Jiang Jieshi) (1888–1975)
    New Life Movement (mid-1930s)
People's Republic, 1949–
    Mao Zedong (1893–1976)
    Cultural Revolution (1966–76)
    Deng Xiaoping (1904–97)
    Establishment of Confucius Institutes (2004)

Chapter 1

Confucius (551–479 BCE) and his legacy: An introduction

Confucius (孔子) lived in the sixth century BCE. Given a choice, however, he would have preferred to live five hundred years earlier, at the dawn of the Zhou dynasty (1045?–221 BCE). It was, he imagined, a golden age, a time when rulers governed through moral example, people practiced time-honored rituals, and social harmony prevailed throughout the land. Much had changed since. No longer was China unified under a virtuous and powerful Zhou king. By 700 BCE the country had splintered into small, independent, and often warring states, ruled over by feudal lords whose authority was maintained not through moral behavior and genuine concern for the welfare of the people but through laws, punishments, and force.

Confucius's preoccupation with the early Zhou was lifelong. If good government, proper social relations, and respectful treatment of one's fellow human beings—all expressed through correct ritual performance—had prevailed then, he was confident that they could be made to prevail again in his own lifetime. To that end, he traveled from one feudal state to another, hoping to find a receptive ruler who, sharing his views, would appoint him to a position of authority where he could put his sociopolitical vision into practice. But his travels were in vain; he never won meaningful employment.

1. A Tang dynasty (618–907) portrait of Confucius carved on a stone stele

Rulers of the day apparently found his ideas impracticable. After all, warfare among the competing states was constant in the sixth century; the message that governing by moral example could triumph in the face of tens of thousands of enemy troops stationed at the borders probably held little persuasive power. It is likely, too, that the Master's personality did not readily win over the feudal rulers. As his teachings in the *Analects* indicate, he could at times be complimentary, sympathetic, tolerant of mistakes, and humorous, but he would often be critical, uncompromising, sarcastic, and harsh.

Confucius, however, never entirely gave up the hope that some ruler somewhere would appreciate the true value of his political teachings. His disciple Zigong once asked, "'If you possessed a piece of beautiful jade, would you hide it away in a locked box, or would you try to sell it at a good price?' The Master [as he is known] responded, 'Oh, I would sell it! I would sell it! I am just waiting for the right offer'" (9.13). Forever disappointed that the right offer never came, Confucius turned his life's work from politics to the teaching of his disciples, men he hoped would embrace his political ideals and go on to succeed in official life where he himself had failed. Traditional accounts put the number of Confucius's serious disciples at seventy-two.

It is a tribute not only to his success as a teacher but, equally, to the dedication of his disciples and later generations of followers that his name holds the place in history that it does. For it is their records of Confucius's sayings and conversations that form the basis of the *Lunyu* (論語), the *Analects*, our main source for Confucius's thought. A text in twenty brief, so-called books—we might understand them better as chapters—totaling roughly five hundred passages or "verses," the *Analects* is a collection of the Master's teachings as recorded by his disciples and edited over the course of generations. It was only in the second century BCE, three centuries after Confucius's death, that the text of the *Analects* achieved its present form.

Any study of the thought of Confucius should begin with this relatively short text. But Confucius came to be closely associated with other early texts in the Chinese tradition as well, especially the *Book of Changes*, the *Book of Odes*, the *Book of History*, the *Book of Rites*, and the *Spring and Autumn Annals*. Beginning in the second century BCE, the Master's followers would claim that Confucius had a role in writing, editing, or compiling each of these five texts (all compiled sometime between roughly 1000 BCE and 200 BCE). Although this claim has not stood up under critical scrutiny, these texts, known as the Five Classics, have been regarded as canonical in the Confucian tradition ever since. Confucians revere them as works that convey principles of sage government, descriptions of proper ritual practice, beliefs about the organization of the cosmos and humankind's relationship to it, and lessons from the history of the Spring and Autumn period (722–481 BCE), perfectly in accord with the Master's teachings.

The rise of Confucianism in China

To say that Confucius gathered around him a group of devoted disciples is not to say that his teachings won universal acclaim immediately. In the highly unstable centuries of the Zhou dynasty known as the Spring and Autumn era and the Warring States period (403–221 BCE), many thinkers, with a wide range of agendas, rose to address the urgent problems of the day. The teachings of Daoists, Legalists, Yin-Yang cosmologists, Diplomatists, Military Strategists, Agriculturalists, Moists (followers of Mozi), and Logicians, among others, all asked: What makes for an effective ruler? What makes for an effective government? What is the ideal relationship between the government and the people? How can China achieve the unity, stability, and prosperity it once knew? What are the responsibilities of the individual, to his family, his community, his state? What is man's place in the cosmos?

Of course, not every thinker gave equal weight to all of these matters. But these were the general concerns that preoccupied what have come to be known as the "hundred schools of thought" that flourished during the Spring and Autumn era and the Warring States period. Vigorous intellectual debate marked these centuries, as thinkers representing the different schools vied to persuade rulers and the intelligentsia of the rightness of their respective teachings. Although Confucianism had especially lively and prominent representatives during these centuries, most notably Mencius (孟子) (fourth c. BCE) and Xunzi (荀子) (third c. BCE), we need to be reminded that Confucian teachings were not yet strongly favored over the teachings of any other thinkers.

That would change by the second century BCE, as Han (202 BC–222 CE) rulers lent increasing support to Confucian teachings. At the dynasty's outset, however, the prospects for these teachings did not appear bright. The Han founder, Liu Bang, was contemptuous of Confucianism. The *Records of the Historian*, written in the first century BCE by Sima Qian, describes the future ruler's early hostility toward the learning of Confucians: "Whenever a visitor wearing a Confucian hat comes to see him, he immediately snatches the hat from the visitor's head and pisses in it, and when he talks to other people, he always curses them up and down."

Having established the Han dynasty, however, Liu Bang (now Emperor Gaozu, r. 202–195 BCE) eventually found it expedient to soften his attitude. In meetings with his principal advisor, Lu Jia, Lu repeatedly urged him to look to the Confucian teachings found in the great classical texts, the *Book of Odes* and *Book of History*, for guidance in governance. One day, clearly tiring of Lu's too frequent admonitions, the emperor responded brusquely: "All I possess I have won on horseback! Why should I bother with the *Book of Odes* and *Book of History*?" Persevering, probably at considerable personal risk, Lu answered:

Your Majesty may have won the empire on horseback, but can you rule it on horseback? ... Qin [the short-lived dynasty replaced by the Han and notorious for its harshness] entrusted its future solely to punishments and law, without changing with the times, and thus eventually brought about the destruction of its ruling family. If, after it had united the world under its rule [in 221 BCE], Qin had practiced benevolence and righteousness and modeled its ways upon the sages of antiquity, how would Your Majesty ever have been able to win possession of the empire?

Gaozu was sufficiently intrigued that he asked Lu Jia to write a book (*Xinyu*, New Discourses) expanding on these ideas. Sima Qian writes that "as each section was presented to the throne, the emperor never failed to express his delight and approval, and all those about him cried, 'Bravo!'"

But it was not until half a century later, during the long reign of Emperor Wu of the Han (r. 141–87 BCE), that Confucian scholars were able, decisively, to promote the teachings of their school and give Confucianism a privileged status at the court, a status that (with some ups and downs) it held until the early years of the twentieth century. Urged by his ministers to elevate Confucianism and abandon the two other major teachings of the day, Daoism and Legalism, the emperor in 141 BCE decreed that all non-Confucians, especially those with Legalist orientations, be dismissed from office. A few years later, in 136 BCE, he established the institution of the "Erudites of the Five Classics," a group expert in the five texts that scholars of the Confucian school had begun to regard as their canonical works—the *Book of Changes*, the *Book of Odes*, the *Book of History*, the *Book of Rites*, and the *Spring and Autumn Annals*. These erudites served as his advisors, drawing on the teachings and principles in the Five Classics in counseling him. In 124 BCE, these same erudites would become the teaching staff at the newly created Imperial Academy. Students who performed well there—who passed examinations demonstrating expertise in one

6

or more of the Five Classics—would win appointment to the official bureaucracy.

The significance of these steps, which will be taken up in some detail in chapter 6, can hardly be overstated. From this time on, Confucianism served as the essential ideological prop of the imperial Chinese state. Rulers would rely on Confucian teachings for guidance and legitimacy, and recruit their bureaucracy through Confucian-based examinations. And, as a consequence of the ideological dominance of Confucianism in government, education in imperial China would center on mastery of Confucian writings. The great prestige—and economic rewards—associated with government service ensured that those who could afford schooling devoted their efforts to the mastery of those texts that would earn them examination success and thus official position. Boys from the age of six or seven would be expected to devote themselves to the study and memorization of primers incorporating Confucian values and then the Confucian Classics. The result: virtually all literate Chinese, particularly during the millennium leading up to the end of imperial China in 1912, were Confucian-schooled and Confucian-socialized. Thus the lives and work of almost all educated Chinese, not just officials but poets, essayists, novelists, artists, calligraphers, historians, scholars, teachers, and the small percentage of literate women were shaped, to one degree or another, by the beliefs and ideals embodied in Confucian texts.

The influence of Confucianism in East Asia

The influence of Confucianism did not stop at China's borders. Although this short introduction focuses on the role of Confucianism in China, we should appreciate that over the course of the centuries, Korea and Japan would find in Confucianism teachings and ideals that, with adaptation, would speak to their social, political, and spiritual needs.

As early as 372, the Korean kingdom of Koguryŏ set up a Confucian academy where the sons of the nobility would be instructed in the Confucian Classics. A few centuries later (682), the Silla kingdom, following Koguryŏ's precedent, established a national Confucian academy for the training of officials; and in 788 it instituted a rudimentary examination system based on the Confucian classics. Under the Koryŏ (918–1392) kings, the examination system expanded; examinations to recruit officials were held more regularly, and the requirements for them now included not only the Classics themselves but also mastery of Chinese commentary on the Classics.

The growing influence of Confucianism peaked in the Chosŏn dynasty (1362–1910). Urged by Confucian reformers, the founders themselves embarked on the task of creating a model Confucian society by restructuring the value system and social practices inherited from the Koryŏ. They set up a nationwide Confucian-based school system and recruited as officials only those who had succeeded in the examination system, which served as the foundation of the Chosŏn Confucian state.

Korea also played an important role in the transmission of Chinese texts to Japan. Korean scholars began bringing these texts, including the *Analects* of Confucius, to Japan as early as the fifth or sixth century. In 604 Prince Shôtoku issued Japan's first "constitution," the so-called Seventeen Article Constitution. Confucian influence is apparent throughout. Article 1 begins by citing directly from the *Analects* (1.12), "Harmony should be valued," and article 4 exhorts ministers and officials to practice proper ritual behavior (*li*, 禮), reminding them that should they abandon the rites, the people will be disorderly. Throughout much of Japanese history the teachings of Buddhism and Shintō would overshadow those of the Confucian school. But in the Tokugawa period (1603–1868), the Confucian school prospered as never before. Japanese scholars, exposed to strains of

Confucianism that had developed in China between the eleventh and sixteenth centuries (see chap. 5, "The Teachings of Neo-Confucianism"), now opened up academies and schools to instruct others. And they lectured to Tokugawa shoguns, urging them to embrace Confucian teachings, which, they argued, could serve as the moral basis of Japanese government and society.

Although Confucianism was promoted as the state learning by the Tokugawa shoguns, it never quite became the exclusive orthodoxy it had been in Chosŏn Korea or China since the tenth century. It may be that in Japan, where a civil service examination system never developed, there was simply more intellectual freedom and space for Buddhism, Shintō, and other currents of thought to flourish. Still, Confucian teachings enjoyed enormous popularity and success in the Tokugawa period, and did much to reshape Japanese ethics and social relations.

Vietnam, too, felt the influence of Confucianism. In 111 BCE, during the Han dynasty, China annexed the region of northern Vietnam, ruling over it for more than a millennium until 939 CE, when Vietnam finally gained its independence. During these many centuries, Chinese culture—in the form of the Chinese writing system, Confucian texts and rituals, and Chinese-style administration—infiltrated Vietnamese life. As part of the Middle Kingdom, the region was also introduced to the Confucian-based Chinese civil service examination system (see chap. 6, "Confucianism in practice"). Even after winning independence in the tenth century, Vietnamese dynasties continued to rely on Confucian examinations to recruit court officials until the 1910s. The prominence of the examination system ensured that into the twentieth century (1) Confucian texts would be the core of the country's educational curriculum; and (2) the educated and political elite would champion values and practices associated with Confucian teachings.

The vision of Confucius

Confucius imagined a future where social harmony and sage rulership would once again prevail. It was a vision of the future that looked heavily to the past. Convinced that a golden age had been fully realized in China's known history, Confucius thought it necessary to turn to that history, to the political institutions, the social relations, the ideals of personal cultivation that he believed prevailed in the early Zhou period, in order to piece together a vision to serve for all times. Here a comparison with Plato, who lived a few decades after the death of Confucius, is instructive. Like Confucius, Plato was eager to improve on contemporary political and social life. But unlike Confucius, he did not believe that the past offered up a normative model for the present. In constructing his ideal society in the *Republic*, Plato resorted much less to reconstruction of the past than to philosophical reflection and intellectual dialogue with others.

This is not to say, of course, that Confucius did not engage in philosophical reflection and dialogue with others. But it was the past, and learning from it, that especially consumed him. This learning took the form of studying received texts, especially the *Book of Odes* and the *Book of History*. He explains to his disciples: "The *Odes* can be a source of inspiration and a basis for evaluation; they can help you to get on with others and to give proper expression to grievances. In the home, they teach you about how to serve your father, and in public life they teach you about how to serve your lord" (17.9). The frequent references to verses from the *Odes* and to stories and legends from the *History* indicate Confucius's deep admiration for these texts in particular and the values, the ritual practices, the legends, and the institutions recorded in them.

But books were not the sole source of Confucius's knowledge about the past. The oral tradition was a source of instructive ancient lore for him as well. Myths and stories about the legendary sage kings Yao, Shun, and Yu; about Kings Wen and Wu and the Duke of Zhou, who founded the Zhou and inaugurated an age of extraordinary social and political harmony; and about famous or infamous rulers and officials like Bo Yi, Duke Huan of Qi, Guan Zhong, and Liuxia Hui—all mentioned by Confucius in the *Analects*—would have supplemented what he learned from texts and served to provide a fuller picture of the past.

Still another source of knowledge for Confucius, interestingly, was the behavior of his contemporaries. In observing them, he would select out for praise those manners and practices that struck him as consistent with the cultural norms of the early Zhou and for condemnation those that in his view were contributing to the Zhou decline. The *Analects* shows him railing against clever speech, glibness, ingratiating appearances, affectation of respect, servility to authority, courage unaccompanied by a sense of right, and single-minded pursuit of worldly success—behavior he found prevalent among contemporaries and that he identified with the moral deterioration of the Zhou. To reverse such deterioration, people had to learn again to be genuinely respectful in dealing with others, slow in speech and quick in action, trustworthy and true to their word, openly but gently critical of friends, families, and rulers who strayed from the proper path, free of resentment when poor, free of arrogance when rich, and faithful to the sacred three-year mourning period for parents, which to Confucius's great chagrin, had fallen into disuse. In sum, they had to relearn the ritual behavior that had created the harmonious society of the early Zhou.

That Confucius's characterization of the period as a golden age may have been an idealization is irrelevant. Continuity with a "golden age" lent his vision greater authority and legitimacy, and such continuity validated the rites and practices he advocated. This desire for historical authority and legitimacy—during a period of disrupture and chaos—may help to explain Confucius's eagerness to present himself as a mere transmitter, a lover of the ancients (7.1). Indeed, the Master's insistence on mere transmission notwithstanding, there can be little doubt that from his study and reconstruction of the early Zhou period he forged an innovative—and enduring—sociopolitical vision. Still, in his presentation of himself as reliant on the past, nothing but a transmitter of what had been, Confucius established what would become something of a cultural template in China. Grand innovation that broke entirely with the past was not much prized in the pre-modern Chinese tradition. A Jackson Pollack who consciously and proudly rejected artistic precedent, for example, would not be acclaimed the creative genius in China that he was in the West. Great writers, great thinkers, and great artists were considered great precisely because they had mastered the tradition—the best ideas and techniques of the past. They learned to be great by linking themselves to past greats and by fully absorbing their styles and techniques. Of course, mere imitation was hardly sufficient; imitation could never be slavish. One had to add something creative, something entirely of one's own, to mastery of the past.

Thus when you go into a museum gallery to view pre-modern Chinese landscapes, one hanging next to another, they appear at first blush to be quite similar. With closer inspection, however, you find that this artist developed a new sort of brush stroke, and that one a new use of ink-wash, and this one a new style of depicting trees and their vegetation. Now that your eye is becoming trained, more sensitive, it sees the subtle differences in the landscape paintings, with their range of masterful techniques and expression. But even as it sees the differences, it recognizes that the paintings evolved out of a common landscape tradition, in which artists built consciously on the achievements of past masters.

Assumptions behind the vision

In forging his vision of a perfectly harmonious society and sage government, Confucius brought with him, as all major thinkers do, a set of assumptions—a worldview that he had been born into and that did much to condition his vision. At its core, Confucius believed, the universe comprised two realms: the human realm and the realm of heaven and earth (the natural realm). In contrast to the human realm, where he assumed order must be actively created and nurtured by human agency (through the practice of ritual), the realm of heaven and earth has an inherent rhythm and harmony that maintain—spontaneously—a perfect balance among its parts. A sort of organic interconnectedness of all being exists. Indeed, one important function of ritual practice in the *Analects* is to ensure that human activity and activity in the realm of heaven and earth are mutually responsive and sustaining.

Thus in Confucius's cosmological outlook, there is no God—that is, there is no monotheistic creator deity, nor any being or entity responsible for the creation of the universe or for its ongoing operation. The cosmos operates on its own, automatically, as it were, and so it has since the beginning of time. It is not that a spirit world populated by nature deities and ancestors does not exist for Confucius and his contemporaries; various spirits could assist human beings in controlling rivers and fields, villages and cities, and families and lineages. But there is no ultimate, omnipotent spirit or deity responsible for the creation of all that is and was. In fact, nowhere in the indigenous Chinese tradition is there textual or archaeological evidence of a belief in what might be called a creator deity. The contrast here with dominant Western monotheistic beliefs is sufficiently striking that some scholars speak about a "cosmological gulf" separating Chinese civilization from Western civilization.

While there is no God or monotheistic creator deity in the *Analects*, the text does make reference to *tian* (天), a concept appearing earlier in the *Book of History* and *Book of Odes*, where, most scholars believe, it refers to a sort of sky-god or a deified ancestor of the Zhou people. The term has come to be conventionally translated as "heaven." The Master, in remarks to disciples, speaks of this *tian* or heaven as understanding him, as

13

recognizing his special qualities—even as rulers of his day might not (14.35); as protecting him when he is briefly imprisoned by the men of Kuang (9.5) and again when Huan Tui attempts to assassinate him (7.23); and as abandoning him when his favorite disciple, Yan Hui, dies (11.9). Thus in most of its appearances in the *Analects*, heaven, although not the all-powerful creator God we find in the West, is an entity possessed of a consciousness and invested in the affairs of the human world. That this heaven can also offer moral guidance to man is clear in 2.4, where the Master comments that at the age of fifty he had finally come to understand "heaven's decree."

The cosmos, Confucius thus assumed, operated of its own, effortlessly achieving a balanced (and moral) harmony among its parts. It was the human realm that needed active regulation. Politics and morality had by his time fallen into a wretched state. The normative sociopolitical order of the early Zhou—what Confucius and his followers called the Dao (道) or Way—had given way to chaos and disorder. Daoists also speak of the Dao or Way, but Confucians and Daoists imbue the term with different meanings. For Daoists, the Way is much grander than the sociopolitical order; indeed, for them it subsumes the sociopolitical order—even heaven and earth. The first chapter of the Daoist classic, the *Daodejing*, refers to it as "the mother of all things." But, although the good order no longer prevailed, it was Confucius's deepest hope and fervent belief that it could be made to prevail again. The Way, he assumed, could be restored, but the restoration project would require the effort of good and righteous men.

Conclusion: Reading the *Analects of Confucius*

Reading the *Analects* for the first time can be challenging, as there is no apparent surface logic to it. After all, the *Analects* is not a sustained text the Master put to writing in his study but rather a collection of his sayings edited over generations by others. The reader thus can find a comment by Confucius on ruling by virtue followed by one about how a child should behave toward his parents, which in turn can be followed by one that speaks to the equal importance of studying and thinking. But, however disparate-seeming they may be, I would suggest that all five hundred or so passages, directly or indirectly, address one of two concerns: (1) what makes for a good man; and (2) what makes for good government. These are for Confucius inseparable matters. Government can be good, as he understands "good," only if good people serve in it. At the same time, it is government by virtue and moral example that leads those it governs to goodness and harmonious human relations. If the reader keeps in mind these two overarching, related concerns—what makes for a good person and what makes for a good government—the coherence underlying the text and the Master's teachings should become clear.

Chapter 2

The individual and self-cultivation in the teachings of Confucius

> There is a common saying among the people: "The empire, the state, and the family": the foundation of the empire lies with the state; the foundation of the state lies with the family; the foundation of the family lies with the person.
>
> (*Mencius* 4A.5)

A moral vanguard of individuals is called for by Confucius and his followers. These individuals move others to proper behavior through the power of their example. By practicing the rituals and respecting the mutual responsibilities required to sustain the so-called five relationships—father–son, ruler–subject, husband–wife, older brother–younger brother, and friend–friend—they provide a model for those around them to follow and thereby bring harmony to family, community, and empire.

The prominent role played by the individual in creating the good sociopolitical order explains why Confucian teachings, throughout the ages, give such profound attention to the process of self-cultivation. Each and every human being is urged to engage in a process of moral refinement, as each and every human being has the capability to exercise a beneficial moral force over others. The *Great Learning*, one of the Confucian classics, puts it straightforwardly: "From the Son of Heaven on down to

論語卷之一　　朱熹集注

學而第一　此爲書之首篇故所記多務本之意乃入道之門積德之基學者之先務也。凡十六章。

子曰學而時習之不亦說乎。說悅同○學之爲言效也。人性皆善而覺有先後後覺者必效先覺之所爲乃可以明善而復其初也。習鳥數飛也。學之不已如鳥數飛也。說喜意也。既學而又時時習之則所學者熟而中心喜說其進自不能已矣。程子曰習重習也。時復思繹浹洽於中則說也。又曰學者將以行之也。時習之則所學者在我故說。謝氏曰時習者無時而不習坐如尸坐時習也立如齊立時習也。

有朋自遠方來不亦樂乎。樂音洛○朋同類也。自遠方來則近者可知。程子曰以善及人而信從者衆故可樂。又曰說在心樂主發散在外。

人不知而不慍不亦君子乎。慍紆問反○慍含怒意。君子成德之名。尹氏曰學在己知不知在人何慍之有。

〔中華書局聚〕

commoners, all without exception should regard self-cultivation as the root." Confucian teachings, then, oblige all followers, irrespective of social, political, and economic status, to take self-cultivation as the starting point in their pursuit of the true Way. It is the basis, "the root" of the devoted Confucian's endeavor to regenerate civility, harmony, and ritual elegance in Chinese society.

The goal for the individual in undertaking the self-cultivation process is to become a *junzi* (君子). *Junzi* is a term that by Confucius's time already had a long history. Made up of two characters, it meant literally, "ruler's son," and referred traditionally to the aristocratic nobility of the Zhou. To be a *junzi* was to be born into the sociopolitical elite; it was a hereditary status, a matter of bloodline. Confucius appropriated the term, giving it a decidedly new twist. In his usage, it came to refer to a person of moral—not sociopolitical—nobility. A *junzi* for Confucius is the *morally* superior person who, by according with the ritual code of the tradition, treats others with respect and dignity, and pursues virtues like humility, sincerity, trustworthiness, righteousness, and compassion.

Throughout the *Analects*, Confucius contrasts this morally superior man with the *xiaoren* (小人), "small man." The small man is one who does not abide by the conventions of decorum and does not choose to follow the moral path. He is *morally* small. On one occasion Confucius baldly distinguishes between the two: "The Master said, 'The superior man [*junzi*] understands righteousness; the small man [*xiaoren*] understands profit'" (4.16). An important shift is taking place in the *Analects* with Confucius's recharacterization of the *junzi*. Whereas earlier a person could not strive to become a *junzi*—one was born into *junzi* status or not—now anyone, at least theoretically, could attain the status through successful self-cultivation. Here Confucius lays down a novel challenge to his contemporaries: through effort, any one of you can *become* a noble person.

The role of learning

Foundational to the self-cultivation process, to becoming a *junzi*, is learning. This perhaps explains why the very opening line of the *Analects* exclaims, "The Master said, 'To learn something and rehearse it constantly, is this indeed not a pleasure?'" (1.1). In comments scattered throughout the rest of the *Analects*, Confucius remarks autobiographically that if there is anything that differentiates him from others it is simply his fondness for learning: "The Master said, 'In a hamlet of ten households, there are sure to be those who in loyalty and trustworthiness are my equal, but none who are my equal in love of learning'" (5.28). This devotion to learning is precisely what separates him from others and makes him a moral example for them.

Consistent with his view that anyone could become a *junzi*, Confucius argues that learning should be open to all. There are to be no social or economic barriers: "In instruction there are to be no distinctions of status" (15.39). Of his own teaching he remarks: "Never have I refused instruction to one who of his own accord comes to me, though it be with as little as a bundle of dried meat." It is the Master's conviction that any person possessed of a genuine eagerness to learn, regardless of status, can hope to improve morally, even to attain "superior man" status.

Scholars have been quick—and right—to point out that while Confucius may have advocated that learning be open to all, in practice few people in his day could have entertained the prospect of receiving the sort of education he proposed. It was simply too costly for much of the Chinese population, most of whom were peasants living close to subsistence. Few families could afford to give up a son's pair of hands around the family plot; if they could, they would next be obliged to pay for supplies—brushes, ink, paper, and texts available at that time only in editions written out laboriously by hand at considerable expense; finally, since education was not sponsored by the state, merely becoming literate typically necessitated the services of a teacher, who required "gifts" or payments from each pupil to support himself.

The Master's willingness to teach anyone who presents himself requires one important qualification: the student has to be genuinely determined (*zhi*, 志) to learn. In thinking back on his own moral trajectory, Confucius marks the starting point of his quest for moral perfection at the age of fifteen when he tells his disciples, "I set (*zhi*) my mind-and-heart on learning." For Confucius to take on a student he must sense a similar passion and commitment: "Those not excited I do not instruct; those not eager I do not enlighten. If I raise up one corner and they do not come back with three corners, I do not continue" (7.8). Confucius presumably is drawing on his own experience. Learning, he knows, can be difficult and the path long. Success demands desire and perseverance. It also demands true engagement and intellectual initiative.

Learning, for Confucius, is learning about the past, about the ancients and their ritual practices, their music, their social and political institutions, and their normative relationships. This past is a reservoir of historical experience in which the "empirical data" for what makes a good order—and what does not—can be found. Because he himself has been so inspired, so deeply affected, by the *Book of History* and the *Book of Odes* in particular, Confucius makes them the basis of his instruction, urging his disciples to read them with the utmost care (e.g., 1.15, 2.2, 2.21, 14.40, 16.13, 17.9, 17.10).

Learning, Confucius cautions, must never become simply a matter of accumulating knowledge: "The Master said, 'Si [disciple Zigong], you think I am the kind of person who learns many things and remembers them, do you not?' He replied, 'Yes, I do. Is that not the case?' The Master replied, 'No, it is not the case. I have one thread that runs through it all'"(15.3). Learning about rituals, music, institutions, proper relationships, and history can easily produce nothing but a list of details and facts. One needs a comprehensive framework that gives coherence to everything one has learned. The particulars acquired through learning hold little significance unless bound together by a totalistic vision, the "one thread."

The good student is therefore expected to build on his learning inferentially, from bits of knowledge to a more comprehensive understanding. Take, for example, Confucius's favorite disciple, Yan Hui. It is, in part, Yan Hui's exceptional inferential powers that explain Confucius's special affection for him: "The Master said to Zigong, 'Of you and Hui, who is the better?' He responded, 'Me? How could I dare compare myself to Hui? Hui hears one matter and understands ten; I hear one matter and understand two.' The Master said, 'No, you are not his equal. Neither of us is his equal'" (5.9). Further, the good student should know how to apply his inferential knowledge. "The Master said, 'Imagine a person who can recite the three hundred poems by heart but when entrusted with matters of governing cannot carry them out, or when sent on a mission to one of the four quarters is unable to exercise his own initiative. No matter how many poems he might have memorized, what good are they to him?'" (13.5). The message here is that book learning that devolves into mere memorization is sterile and useless and not the true learning that will enable self-transformation and the betterment of society.

By "learning," then, Confucius means moral learning, the study and embodiment of the values that will make one a *junzi*, a superior man. He laments that in his own day learning has been reduced to nothing more than a means to worldly success or acclaim: "In ancient times those who learned did so for the sake of bettering themselves; nowadays those who learn do so for the sake of impressing others" (14.24). His aim is to get men back on the right track, to make learning once again about moral self-improvement.

The Master's insistence that the Confucian responsibility to pursue moral perfection, or sagehood, must be rooted in a steadfast commitment to learning is in large part based on his own life experience. In the famous "autobiographical" passage in the *Analects*, he states:

> At fifteen, I set my mind-and-heart on learning. At thirty, I stood on my own. At forty, I had no doubts. At fifty, I knew heaven's decree. At sixty, my ears were in accord. At seventy, I followed the desires of my mind-and-heart without overstepping right. (2.4)

Though autobiographical, the remark is clearly intended to serve as a sequential template for all students of the Confucian school. The path to moral perfection, it counsels, must start with an unswerving commitment to learning. Through learning, a student, too, might become a sage—a man whose every action is instinctively in line with the Way.

Being a morally superior man: true goodness through ritual practice

Although the *Analects* does not offer up one neat definition of the morally superior man, it does in passage after passage introduce his various attributes. Most importantly, the morally superior man is a man of *ren* (仁). *Ren* is the highest virtue in the Confucian vision, the one that subsumes all others, including trustworthiness, righteousness, compassion, ritual propriety, wisdom, and filial piety. No translation quite captures the full significance of the term. It has been variously rendered as "benevolence," "humanity," "humanness," and the like; I translate it as "true goodness" here, hoping that this translation conveys something of *ren*'s overarching, paramount status in Confucius's teachings.

True goodness is not a quality that can be cultivated in seclusion, cut off from other human beings. True goodness exists only as it is manifested in relation to others and in the treatment of others.

It is in concrete behavior that true goodness, as a virtue, is achieved. A filial son, for instance, "enacts" his filial devotion by bowing before his father. True goodness is thus closely associated with ritual, for it is principally through the practice of ritual, the Master believes, that true goodness is given meaningful expression. For this reason, we find the Master dedicating much of his teaching in the *Analects* to a discussion of proper ritual. To be morally superior, Confucius argues, is to have a keen sense of ritual propriety.

On true goodness

As crucial as the concept of true goodness may be for Confucius, he never provides a synoptic explanation or definition of his supreme virtue. This frustrates his disciples, who dog him throughout the *Analects* with questions like: "What is true goodness?" "Is so-and-so a man of true goodness?" "Is such-and-such behavior a matter of true goodness?" The Master's answers are varied and appear to depend on to whom and about whom he is speaking. True goodness can be to love others (12.22), to subdue the self and return to ritual propriety (12.1), to be respectful, tolerant, trustworthy, diligent, and kind (17.5), to be possessed of courage (14.4), to be free from worry (9.29), or to be resolute and firm (13.27). What Confucius offers by way of explanation to his disciples are but glimpses or facets of true goodness. Aware of their frustration and eagerness for fuller disclosure, he remarks, "My friends, I know you think that there is something I am keeping from you. But I keep nothing from you at all" (7.23). True goodness, it would seem, is not fully expressible, fully definable. There is an ineffable quality to it.

It remains for us—as it did for his followers—to tease out of the *Analects* a deeper appreciation of this essential moral quality. A few passages in the text are especially revealing: "Zigong asked, 'Is there one word that can be practiced for the whole of one's life?' The Master said, 'That would be 'empathy' perhaps: what you do not wish yourself do not do unto others'" (15.24). True goodness lies in the direction of empathetic behavior. In dealing with others, we are obliged to treat them as we ourselves would wish to be treated. We need to put ourselves in their place, to plumb our own feelings, in order to judge the feelings of others; this is Confucian empathy. True goodness is realized when these feelings of empathy are successfully extended to others, when they are actualized in our relations with others: "The Way of our Master is being true to oneself and empathetic toward others, nothing more" (4.15).

It may be rather easy to be empathetic at any one particular moment or in any one particular encounter. The difficulty, Confucius suggests, lies in sustaining the feelings and the practice of empathy over the course of an entire day as we interact with a variety of people, from concerned student to grieving friend to demanding child to sickly neighbor to aggressive panhandler to distraught colleague to exhausted spouse. And if an entire day poses a challenge, more challenging still is an entire week or an entire month. This perhaps explains why Confucius resists describing anyone, including himself, as a man of true goodness (7.43). For the very moment one's empathetic feelings and practice lapse, so too does one's true goodness. Yan Hui does better than most at sustaining true goodness but even his success is limited: "The Master said, 'Hui! For three months his mind-and-heart would not lapse from true goodness. As for others, they might attain it for a day or for a month, but that is all'"(6.7). Thus it is important to recognize that true goodness is not an indwelling state that one achieves once and for all; it is a *behavior* involving mind and body that is ongoing and requires constant vigilance. This is why Zengzi, another of Confucius's foremost disciples, remarks, "A learned man must be broad and resolute, for his burden is heavy and the journey is long. He takes true goodness as his burden: Is that not indeed heavy? And only with death does he stop: Is that not indeed long?" (8.7). In the Confucian tradition, being a superior man, a man of true goodness, requires a lifelong commitment that ceases only with death itself.

The etymology of the Chinese character for true goodness is itself instructive. *Ren* (仁) is constituted of two components, one for "man" and the other for "two," indicating that a person can be *ren*—truly good—only in associating with others. True goodness in the Confucian tradition is not a quality that can be cultivated and expressed in isolation. There is no place in Confucianism for the Semitic tradition's "athlete of God," who sits atop a forty-foot pillar in the Syrian desert cultivating goodness and ridding himself of evil in the eyes of God. True goodness for Confucius is inter-relational, a virtue given realization only in a person's interactions with other human beings.

On ritual

Confucius insists in the *Analects* that the superior man's empathetic concerns are necessarily both guided by and expressed through a set of *li* (禮) (conventionally translated as rituals or ritual propriety, but rendered also as rites, ceremonies, prescriptions for proper behavior, rules of etiquette, and customs) handed down by the tradition and refined over the centuries. Yet, as in the case of true goodness, he does not attempt to define ritual for his disciples or offer a general explanation of its significance and function. Turning to the later *Book of Rites*, however, we find some helpful passages. For instance:

> Now, ritual furnishes the means of determining the observance towards relatives, as near and remote; of settling points that may cause suspicion or doubt; of distinguishing where there should be agreement and disagreement; and of making clear what is right and what is wrong. In practicing ritual, one does not seek to please others in an improper way or to be lavish in one's words. In practicing ritual one does not go beyond the proper measure, nor take liberties with others, nor presume an intimacy with others. To cultivate the self and put one's words into practice is what is called good conduct. Conduct that is cultivated, words that accord with the right Way—this is the substance of ritual.

It is the performance of ritual that "humanizes" or "civilizes" man and distinguishes him from beast:

> The parrot can speak, and yet is nothing more than a bird; the ape can speak, and yet is nothing more than a beast. Here now is a man who observes no rules of ritual propriety; is not his mind-and-heart that of a beast? But if men were as beasts, and without the principle of ritual propriety, father and son might have the same mate. Therefore, when the sages arose, they framed the rules of ritual propriety in order to teach men, and cause them, by their possession of them, to make a distinction between themselves and brutes.

Li, or ritual, offers guidance for people in their manifold dealings with others, and it is this guidance that makes social harmony possible. A father, in practicing proper ritual, behaves as a true father should; a son, in practicing proper ritual, behaves as a true son should. Ritual thus promotes the actualization of the normative five relationships. Confucius believes that the good order of the early Zhou had been built on these five relationships and that it is these relationships that constitute the basis of any good sociopolitical order. As the *Book of Rites* states, "Ruler and subject, father and son, husband and wife, elder brother and younger brother, and friend and friend: these five relationships constitute the universal Way of the world."

As a young child, a person begins to learn from family ceremonies how to pay reverence to ancestors, how to mourn the dead, and how to celebrate life's important transitions, like capping—the ceremony representing the coming of age—and marriage. He becomes familiar with how many and which particular ritual vessels to use in sacrificing to his grandfather, and which clothes to wear, prayers to say, and foods to eat during times of mourning. He even knows not to wear purple or mauve-colored adornments or use red or vermillion for informal dress and not to wear a black cap on condolence visits. But for Confucius, ritual practice is not limited to what we may think of as religious or ceremonial occasions; for him, all aspects of life, even the most mundane, are governed by a system of rituals. How we eat, how we speak, how we greet others, how we dress, and how we bear ourselves publicly and privately are matters determined by ritual expectations and tradition. Thus, about eating, the *Book of Rites* admonishes:

> Do not roll the rice into a ball; do not bolt down the various dishes; do not swill down the soup. Do not make noise in eating; do not crunch the bones with the teeth; do not put back fish you've been eating; do not throw the bones to the dogs; do not snatch at what you want. Do not spread out the rice to cool; do not use chopsticks in eating millet. Do not try to gulp down soup with vegetables in it, nor add condiments to it; do not keep picking the teeth, nor swill down the sauces.

To many in the West, these proscriptions may seem trivial—a matter of simple manners or etiquette rather than of moral development. But there is no doubt that Confucius saw them as rituals, the correct performance of which enabled man to nurture and give expression to true goodness: "The instructive and transforming power of rituals is subtle: they stop depravity before it has taken form, causing men daily to move towards what is good and to distance themselves from vice, without being themselves conscious of it."

Of course ritual would have this "instructive and transforming" power only if performed with utter sincerity. The Master worries lest students take ritual practice to be mere performance, gesture empty of meaning. For ritual to have genuine significance, the performance of it must be infused with the proper feeling: "Ritual performed without reverence, the forms of mourning observed without grief—these are things I cannot bear to see!" (3.26). Offerings of wine and food to ancestors must be accompanied by feelings of reverence and affection; bowing before an elder must be accompanied by feelings of respect; polite speech, dress, and meal manners must be accompanied by feelings of propriety and civility toward other human beings. Ritual practice is thus the means by which man gives expression to his most human qualities. It is the means by which his inner feelings and outer demeanor become one.

In the teachings of the *Analects*, ritual practice appears to be at once a means of manifesting our humanity and a means of nurturing within us the very qualities that make us human. Through sacrificial offerings we deepen our feelings of reverence for ancestors; through the act of bowing we deepen our feelings of respect for the elderly; through decorous speech, dress, and meal manners we deepen our feelings of propriety and civility toward others. For Confucius, the physical practice of the rites inculcates in the performer the emotions and feelings associated with those rites. Immersion in the rites, which is what Confucius calls for throughout the *Analects*, habituates man externally to good, normative social behavior, and this habituated behavior guides and reshapes his moral impulses. Once, when asked what constitutes true goodness, the Master replied simply: "If contrary to ritual, do not look; if contrary to ritual, do not listen; if contrary to ritual, do not speak; if contrary to ritual, do not act" (12.1).

For Confucius, ritual is closely linked to music. The capacity of music to inspire moral behavior had been realized long before by the ancients. As the *Book of Rites* states, "In music the sages found pleasure and saw that it could be used to make the hearts of the people good. Because of the deep influence that it exerts on a man, and the change that it produces in manners and customs, the ancient kings appointed it as one of the subjects of instruction." Confucius thus assumes that his followers should study music—or, more precisely, certain types of music he finds morally uplifting—as an essential part of the ritual matrix of the past. He especially recommends Shao music (i.e., the court music of the sage-king Shun), remarking that it has a powerful effect even on himself (3.25, 7.14, 15.11). Music's importance—and its close association with ritual in Confucian teachings—is summed up neatly in this simple exhortation to his disciples: "Find inspiration in the *Book of Odes*, take your place through ritual, and achieve perfection with music" (8.8).

The family as the crucible of virtue

Family clothes and shelters us, but its most important function in Confucian teachings is to set us on the path to virtue. Family is a microcosm of society, the locus for learning about human relationships and the norms that govern them. It is here that, ideally, we are inculcated in those values and practices that make a harmonious Confucian society possible: obedience and respect for authority, deference to seniority, affection and kindness toward the young and infirm, and so forth.

3. A copy (fourteenth century?) of a painting by Li Gonglin (ca. 1041–1106) of a filial son bowing before his parents

The second passage of the *Analects* speaks to the essential role of family in shaping the moral individual and promoting a peaceful and stable social and political order. Youzi, expressing the views of his Master, remarks:

> One who is filial and fraternal but at the same time loves defying superiors is rare indeed. One who does not love defying superiors but at the same time loves sowing disorder has never existed. The superior man attends to the root. When the root is established, the Way issues forth. Filial piety and fraternal respect—are they not the root of true goodness? (1.2)

Moral cultivation of the individual thus begins in the family. This is where a person is introduced to filial piety, fraternal respect, and deference for elders; this is where a person is instructed in the nomenclature of ritual etiquette. The lessons learned here apply readily in the world out there. A good son will naturally be obedient to the ruler; a good younger brother will naturally be respectful to elders; a good daughter and wife will naturally be submissive to men. The pressure on the family to provide the right moral environment is considerable, for a wayward son—one who is disobedient to the village elders or the ruler—brings disrepute not only on himself but his entire family, especially his father and mother. His failure is theirs; as parents they did not engender moral purpose and proprietary awareness in their son, and it is the community that now suffers the consequences.

Of the virtues to be learned in the family, filial piety is the most fundamental. The essence of filial piety is obedience to parental authority: to respect their wishes and to care for their well-being. The *Book of Rites* summarizes the responsibilities associated with this cardinal virtue:

> A filial son, in nourishing his aging parents, seeks to make their hearts glad and not to go against their will; to make their ears and eyes glad and bring comfort to them in their bed-chambers; and to

support them wholeheartedly with food and drink—such is the filial son to the end of life. By "the end of life," I mean not the end of his parents' lives, but the end of his own life. Thus what his parents loved he will love, and what they reverenced he will reverence. He will do so even in regard to all their dogs and horses, and how much more in regard to the men whom they valued.

In Confucian thinking, filial obligations do not cease with the death of the parents. True filiality requires that the child behave throughout his entire life just as his parents would wish and in a fashion that would reflect well on the family's good name:

Although his parents be dead, when a son is inclined to do what is good, he should think that he will thereby transmit the good name of his parents, and carry his wish into effect. When he is inclined to do what is not good, he should think that he will thereby bring disgrace on the name of his parents, and must not carry his wish into effect.

Filial respect thus does not play out within the web of family relations alone but gets actualized in the larger network of social relations as good, virtuous conduct.

What is true of ritual generally is equally true of filial piety more particularly: the feeling behind the form is essential. This message is repeated over and over in Confucian teachings, as in the Master's pointed response to disciple Ziyou's query about filial piety: "Nowadays to be 'filial' means simply to be capable of providing parents with nourishment. But even dogs and horses get their nourishment from us. Without the feeling of reverence, what difference is there?" (2.7). As he does with all ritual practice, Confucius insists that outer filial behavior be the faithful expression of a genuine inner feeling.

The family, in the Confucian vision, is of central importance in sustaining the Chinese sociopolitical order, for it is here, in the family, that the child becomes conditioned to the dominant assumptions and values of Chinese society. From the family the child learns that the world is naturally hierarchical; that hierarchy works effectively when there exist clear status differentiations and clear roles; that each status has set, normative responsibilities attached to it (e.g., there are behavioral norms for being a good son or daughter); that, enmeshed in a hierarchical network, a good person is one who carries out the responsibilities associated with his status; and that harmony of the whole results from each person within the hierarchy conscientiously fulfilling the duties demanded by his defined role.

Chapter 3

Government in Confucian teachings

> Ji Kangzi [the de facto but illegitimate ruler of the state of Lu] asked Confucius about governing. Confucius responded, "To govern (*zheng*, 政) means to correct (*zheng*, 正). If you lead by correcting yourself, who would dare to remain incorrect?" (12.17)

The ruler as exemplar

The cultivation of the individual has as its aim moral self-realization. But, as this remark suggests, self-realization of the individual is by no means an end itself. Self-realization, Confucius believes, results in the self-realization of others, which, ripple-like, can result in the moral transformation of society at large. This, of course, is why the presence of a moral vanguard is so crucial to Confucian teachings—and why Confucius dedicates the time he does to explaining what it means to be good, to be moral, and to become a superior man. Social harmony comes about less through the instrumentation of government than through the power of example set by a moral elite. At the apex of this moral elite, at least ideally, sits the exemplary ruler, who, in his utter correctness, serves as a model for all.

The Confucian ruler possesses an inner virtue (*de*, 德). This inner virtue exerts a spiritual-ethical power over others. People are drawn to it and to him. Confucius offers a comparison to the natural world: "One who practices government by virtue may be compared to the North Star: it remains in its place while the multitude of stars turn toward it" (2.1). The people's submission to the good Confucian ruler clearly is not submission to some coercive power but rather to a fixed, reliable moral authority that radiates throughout the realm. This moral authority is a force capable of guiding others in their movements, of setting them in the right direction. The theme of instructing and ruling the populace through moral suasion runs throughout the *Analects* as well as other classical Confucian texts; indeed, it is one of the distinguishing features of Confucian political philosophy.

Ji Kangzi, cited above, returns to the subject of government on a number of occasions: "Ji Kangzi asked Confucius about government, saying, 'Suppose I were to kill the Way-less in order to promote those possessed of the Way. What would you say?'" With no little hint of impatience and even disdain for the usurper Ji Kangzi, Confucius answered, "You are governing; what need is there for killing? If you desire the good, the people will be good. The virtue of the superior man is wind; the virtue of the small person is grass. When wind passes over it, the grass is sure to bend" (12.19). Ji Kangzi just does not get it. Harsh government that relies on punishment and physical force is ineffective and represents "misgovernment" in Confucius's view. All that is necessary for good government is moral leadership. Morality breeds morality. The wind–grass metaphor that brings the exchange with Ji Kangzi to its conclusion is easily one of the most famous in the Chinese tradition. The people are susceptible to the moral suasion of their ruler. And his influence on them is presented as altogether "natural," just as wind naturally bends the grass. Note here that just as a moral ruler will move the people in the direction of goodness, a ruler lacking in moral authority will move the people in the direction of immorality. Thus in the Confucian tradition, a ruler without virtue poses a serious threat to the entire moral-social order.

So strong is his confidence in the transformative power of virtue, in its ability to win others over to a moral life, that when Confucius once expressed a desire to settle among the Nine Barbarian Tribes of the East and was asked, "But what about their crudeness?" he matter-of-factly replied, "If a superior man were to settle among them, there would be no crudeness" (9.14). With correct moral leadership even "barbarians" would become correct.

A good ruler, Confucius tells Ji Kangzi, simply desires the good himself. He must model the morality he would like his subjects to cultivate. Conversely, when disorderly behavior prevails in a state, the ruler must look within and consider his own culpability: "Ji Kangzi was having trouble with burglars. He asked Confucius what he should do. Confucius answered, 'If only you were free from desire, they would not steal even if you rewarded them for it'" (12.18). If thievery abounds in the state of Lu, the responsibility, Confucius maintains, falls on Ji Kangzi. It is, after all, from the ruler that the people learn morality. If the ruler is good and without avarice, the people, too, will be good and without avarice. That being the case, there is nothing that could induce them to steal. A ruler thus can bring Confucian harmony to his state and people only if he is without selfish desire himself.

If good government depends upon the existence of a moral vanguard, then the responsibility falls to the ruler to identify those individuals whose moral character qualifies them for official service. Choosing the right men is essential: "Duke Ai asked, 'What can be done so that the people will be obedient?' The Master responded, 'Raise up the straight, place them over the crooked, and the people will be obedient; raise up the crooked, place them over the straight, and the people will not be obedient'" (2.19). This passage speaks to a familiar theme: the power of example, the power that the blowing wind naturally exercises over blades of grass. The straight in office will bring correctness to those whom they oversee. But it speaks to another, related point as well. If the ruler is unprejudiced in the selection of his officials, if he bypasses the unqualified and the corrupt and promotes only the good, his commitment to the well-being of his people will be apparent. Observing his dedication to their well-being, the people in turn will continue to offer him their trust and support.

It is this trust, Confucius goes on to say, that is the basis of the state and of the ruler's legitimacy:

> Zigong asked about government. The Master said, "Let food be sufficient, let military preparations be sufficient, and let the people have trust in you." Zigong said, "If you have absolutely no choice but to give up one of the three, which should go first?" He said, "Let the military preparations go." Zigong said, "If you have absolutely no choice but to give up one of the remaining two, which should go first?" "Let the food go. Since ancient times, nobody has escaped death; but if the people lack trust, the government has nothing on which to stand." (12.7)

The implication here is that a people with confidence in their ruler, persuaded that he puts their welfare above all else, will be willing to endure all manner of hardship. His genuine concern for their well-being will be rewarded with their loyalty and support, even when their very lives are at risk.

The good, virtuous ruler is the consummate superior man, always comporting himself as he should. He is the perfect model, according effortlessly with the prescriptions for proper behavior. It is through his charismatic moral example that he instructs and guides his people, and sets them on the right path. In this ideal of rulership, Confucius argues, laws, edicts, and punishments—the routine tools of government—are inessential. It is not to say they are altogether unnecessary, but for the Master, the less dependence on them—and the greater dependence on the person of the ruler, his moral light, and his ritual modeling—the better. Laws and punishments imposed from above may indeed promote a superficial social order among the people, but they do little to inculcate in them a sense of right and to lead them to moral betterment. And they do little to promote a true spirit of community, a mutual commitment by the people to the creation of a harmonious society. Of all the Master's remarks, this one best sums up Confucius's view on the basis of good government:

> Guide them by edicts, keep them in line with punishments, and the common people will stay out of trouble, but will have no sense of shame. Guide them by virtue, keep them in line with ritual and they will, besides having a sense of shame, reform themselves. (2.3)

Moral reformation of the individual, as well as social harmony, do not result from the external threat and coercion of laws and punishments. Instead, they result from the people, inspired by the ruler's model to re-create in the community and state, through ritual practice, the fluid, normative relationships that have formed their familial life since childhood.

Culture and tradition, Confucius suggests here, are more effective, stronger tools in shaping the behavior and ideals of the people than legal and penal codes. Through example and moral suasion, the good ruler promotes a system of shared values and practices, which effectively regulates the conduct of the people and, importantly, binds each person to the community and its norms. Violating these norms has real and sometimes long-lasting consequences, Confucius assumes. A person who uses his fingers rather than chopsticks to eat yellow fish, or curses his elderly father in public, or wears lavish clothing during the mourning period for a parent will likely be branded by others as uncouth and uncivilized. He has failed, after all, to learn what it means to be truly Chinese and now risks being marginalized by his fellow villagers. While no formal laws mete out fines or other penalties for this sort of "misbehavior," the threat of punishment is nonetheless substantial. This is why Confucius is confident that in a society governed by shared culture the people will not be quick to transgress the boundaries of customary behavior and will develop a keen sense of shame.

In leading by ritual, the ruler assumes the role as standard-bearer of the culture, thus enhancing his legitimacy; at the same time, he serves as instructor, exemplifying for the people the beliefs and practices they are expected to embrace as well. Confucius's faith in the efficacy of rule by ritual is evidenced repeatedly in conversations with his disciples: "The Master said, 'If a person is capable of governing the state with ritual and humility, what difficulties will he have? If he is incapable of governing the state with ritual and humility, what does he have to do with ritual?'" (4.13). But ritual is effective *only* if the ruler's practice of it is informed by the proper feeling, the spirit of humility or deference. It is this feeling that gives the ruler's ritual performance authenticity and endows that performance with the power to guide and "reform" (2.3) the people.

It would be a mistake, however, to conclude that Confucius sees no place for law and punishment in government. Despite his appeal for rule by virtue and ritual, he regards penal law as a routine part of the apparatus of government. He says of the superior man, for example, that he "cherishes a respect for the law," in contrast to the small man, who "cherishes lenient treatment" (4.11). And in an exchange with Zilu, he remarks, "If rituals and music do not prosper, punishments and penalties will not be correct; if punishments and penalties are not correct, the people will have no place to put hand or foot" (13.3). Indeed, both the *Book of History* and *Book of Odes*, which Confucius holds so dear, speak of the righteous application of laws and punishments by the virtuous rulers of the early Zhou (e.g., "The Announcement to the Prince of Kang"). He likely appreciates that in order to maintain social order, occasional recourse to laws and punishments is unavoidable. Still, it is clear that he would like their use to be minimized. When he remarks, "In hearing lawsuits I am just like others. What is necessary is to see to it that there are no lawsuits" (12.13), the

Master is stating a central tenet of Confucian teachings: the best government is the one that relies on law least.

The picture of the ideal ruler that emerges from the *Analects* is of a man whose inner virtue radiates outward as a powerful, charismatic, moral force that moves people toward true goodness and the practice of ritual propriety, thus producing social harmony. This force is non-coercive, and its effects seem natural, like grass bending in the direction of the blowing wind. The ideal ruler thus need not even govern actively: "The Master said, 'Ruling through non-action (*wuwei*, 無為), is this not Shun! For what did he do? Assuming a reverential pose, he faced due south and nothing more'" (15.5). Commentators understand this passage to mean that so great, so abundant was the sage-ruler Shun's virtue that he transformed his people effortlessly without taking action; it is an echo of analect 2.1, where the ruler is likened to the North Star "that remains in its place while the multitude of stars turn toward it." Daoists, too, use the term "non-action" to suggest that "action" or "doing" should be spontaneous, not purposeful or in any way contrary to the natural course of things. Commentators distinguish Confucius's use of the term here by giving it moral significance, explaining that "non-action" in Shun's case was possible only because his inner virtue was exceptionally powerful. In other words, "non-action" was a direct consequence of his moral condition. We need also to remember, however, that Shun's "non-action" in the concrete, daily affairs of government was possible only because as a virtuous ruler and in his compassion for the people, he had chosen upright and good men like Gao Yao to carry out the administration of government (12.22).

The good ruler is necessarily a good judge of character and selects as officials only those men who share his commitment to Confucian principles and the well-being of the people. Here we get a hint of why the famous Chinese civil service examination system will take on the importance it does for more than two millennia beginning in the second century BCE.

Government and the well-being of the people

In the Confucian vision, then, the well-being of the people is dependent largely on the moral character of the ruler. The responsibility of actualizing his benevolence in the administration of the realm is shared by him and his appointed officials. Like the ruler himself, the ideal official is expected to be a good man; he is a man who, having undergone the process of self-cultivation, is steeped in learning and dedicated to becoming a morally superior man (*junzi*). Indeed, we have seen that the *Analects* is, in part, an attempt by the Master to teach his students the way of being moral, in the hope that they might succeed where he himself had failed—in achieving official position. Only good people, he believes, can make good officials, and it is only good officials who can make the government good.

A good official is not a person who exercises a particular skill or fulfills a particular function. Indeed, Confucius's terse remark, "The superior man is not a utensil" (2.12), speaks to this ideal. The traditional commentary on this passage by He Yan (fl. third century CE) states: "As for utensils, each is of circumscribed usefulness. But when it comes to the superior man, there is nothing he does not do." The reason that "there is nothing he does not do" is that he embodies virtue. In embodying virtue, he is fully compassionate and benevolent and unfailingly extends himself to others. Through his finely honed empathetic skills, he is poised to deal with the whole gamut of affairs confronting state and society. This is not to say that he might not be especially expert in certain areas, such as irrigation control or taxation or techniques of administration; rather, such specialized skills are not what make him a good official. It is his readiness to improve the lot of the people, to see to their needs as they arise, that makes him a good official.

4. (*Opposite*) **A woodblock print of an official caring for the well-being of his subjects, as his Confucian duty demands. The caption reads, "Open the granaries and provide relief to the distressed." From** *Zhongguo gudian wenxue banhua xuanji*, **ed. by Fu Xihua (1981)**

開倉賑濟

Confucian teachings oblige the superior man to serve government, to assist the ruler in implementing the Way throughout the country. True goodness, after all, lies in serving and bettering others. Yet there are times, according to Confucius, when the superior man can refuse to serve. Of Qu Boyu, a minister in the state of Wei who resigned his post in 559 BCE, the Master exclaims: "A superior man indeed was Qu Boyu! When the Way prevailed in the state, he served it; when the Way did not prevail in the state, he was able to roll up his principles and hide them away" (15.7). And, similarly but more abstractly, the Master says: "When the Way prevails in the world, show yourself; when it does not, hide yourself" (8.13).

Remarks like these seem at odds with the leitmotif running through the *Analects*—that it is the responsibility of the superior man to transform a wayward society and give it moral redirection. How can Confucius permit the superior man to "hide himself" at the very time his presence is most required? Consider too that Confucius is living in a time when the Way certainly does not prevail, and yet, as we have seen in the exchange with Zigong cited earlier (see chap. 1), he still anxiously awaits the "right offer" (9.13). Never does he doubt his own ability to set a benighted ruler and society on the right path, given the opportunity: "The Master said, 'If there were someone to employ me, in the course of but twelve months we would be doing well, and within three years we would achieve success'" (13.10). Serving a ruler, then, is what is *ordinarily* expected of the superior man. But in passages like the ones above, the Master sounds a cautionary note, suggesting that occasionally a state and its ruler may be so hopelessly depraved that they simply are not susceptible to the morally transforming influences of the superior man. In such a state, the superior man has no room or license to act on his principles. In fact, any insistence on doing so will merely invite the ruler's wrath and result in severe punishment. Faced with a ruler hostile to moral reform, the superior man would do better to "roll up his principles and hide them away."

Since good government in the Confucian vision depends largely on the virtue of the ruler and those he appoints to serve him, the teachings of the Master do not offer much in the way of plans for the organization of government or division of governing powers—as one finds, for example, in the U.S. Constitution—or of specific measures or policies the government should adopt. The Master assumes that a moral ruler, out of compassion and benevolence, will do what is right and will take the appropriate steps to address the needs of his subjects.

Still, it is possible to deduce a few general policy suggestions from some passages of the *Analects*. For instance, the Master says, "To guide a state of one thousand chariots, be respectful in your handling of affairs and display trustworthiness; be frugal in your expenditures and cherish others; and employ the common people only at the proper seasons" (1.5). The ruler, according to Confucius, has a responsibility to the people for their material well-being. A government that spends too much is one that is bound to tax too much; government must be fiscally sensitive, mindful of the heavy burden taxation places on the people. Government must be mindful, too, not to draw on the people's labor for public work projects during the agricultural seasons. To interfere with the people's agricultural activities cannot but reduce their agricultural productivity, the basis of their livelihood.

In an exchange with his disciple Ran Qiu, Confucius suggests why the material well-being of the people is a critical concern for the government:

> The Master traveled to Wei, with Ran Qiu as his carriage driver. The Master remarked, "How numerous the people of this state are!" Ran Qiu asked, "Since the people are already numerous, what next should be done for them?" The Master said, "Enrich them." Ran Qiu said, "Once they have become rich, what next should be done for them?" The Master said, "Instruct them." (13.9)

43

The implied claim here is that only when the people's material needs have been satisfied will they be susceptible to moral instruction. In this view, the receptivity of the people to the ruler's charismatic influence depends on socioeconomic conditions, for which the ruler is accountable.

Confucius praises the legendary sage-king Yu for dedicating himself to projects intended to benefit the people's agriculture. The Master says of Yu, "He lived in a mean hovel expending all of his energies on the construction of drainage ditches and canals. I can find no fault with Yu" (8.21). By attempting to tame the constant flooding and improve field irrigation, Yu's government was doing just what government is supposed to do: to promote, to the best of its ability, the agricultural prosperity of the people (cf. 14.5). Agricultural prosperity had long been the concern of Chinese rulers. Indeed, in oracle bone inscriptions from the Shang dynasty (ca. 1600 BCE–ca. 1045 BCE), which represent the earliest recorded history in China, dynastic rulers rarely stop dancing, praying, and performing sacrifices to coax the rain and to ensure bountiful harvests.

The mandate of heaven

The ideal of rule by virtue is by no means new with Confucius. It is a major theme wending its way through many of the early Zhou documents preserved in the *Book of History*.

These documents tell of a Shang dynasty that began virtuously with wise and benevolent rulers. Over time, however, the character of the rulers changed, and men given to great lewdness, debauchery, and wickedness came to occupy the throne. The last of the Shang rulers, King Zhou, was especially depraved, and the descriptions of him in the documents are unrestrained in their contempt for him. In rallying his troops for the Zhou attack on the Shang forces, King Wu, the founder of the Zhou, says:

Now Zhou, the great king of the Shang, does not reverence heaven above and inflicts calamities on the people below. He has been abandoned to drunkenness and reckless in lust. He has dared to exercise cruel oppression. Along with criminals he has punished all their relatives. He has put men into office on the hereditary principle. He has made it his pursuit to have palaces, towers, pavilions, embankments, ponds, and all other extravagances, to the most painful injury of you, the myriad people. He has burned and roasted the loyal and the good. He has ripped up pregnant women. August heaven was moved with indignation, and charged my deceased father Wen reverently to display heaven's majesty, but he died before the work was completed.

King Zhou was not a "good" man and thus not a "good" ruler. Under him, the *Book of History* goes on to say, people lived in abject misery. And so, "wailing and calling to heaven, they fled to where no one could reach them." Heaven, in its compassion, took pity on the people and withdrew the Mandate it had given earlier rulers of the Shang, bestowing it anew on the Zhou.

It is here, with the *Book of History*, that the concept of the Mandate of Heaven (*tianming*, 天命) is first introduced in Chinese history. Attributed to the Duke of Zhou, the righteous regent of the young King Cheng, the Mandate of Heaven would serve as the basis of Chinese political ideology from the Zhou dynasty until the early years of the twentieth century. Curiously, however, though Confucius insists throughout his teachings that virtue alone makes for the good ruler, he does not use the term *tianming* in the sense of the Mandate of Heaven in the *Analects*. It may be that the term did not have especially wide currency yet; conversely, it may have had sufficiently wide currency that he simply assumed his disciples to understand that much of his discussion with them was a sort of commentary on it. Whatever the case, it is certain that his teachings subscribed to and promoted the ideals embodied in the Mandate of Heaven.

The theory of the Mandate, on the face of it, is simple enough. A concerned heaven, a heaven invested in the well-being of the people (see chap. 1), confers a mandate to rule on virtuous and benevolent men who, like heaven, are committed to the people's welfare. Such had been the case with the early rulers of the Shang, according to the *History* documents. To maintain the Mandate, these men—and their successors—must never abandon virtue. If they do, if the rulers go bad, they forfeit the right to rule, and heaven withdraws its Mandate.

What is essential to note here is that heaven does not act on its own; heaven responds to the wishes and will of the people. In "wailing and calling to heaven," the people voice *their* displeasure and discontent with the ruler and with the conditions prevailing in the state. Heaven, to be sure, is a vital force—and a powerful sanction—in the political dynamic, but it is something of an agent operating on behalf of the interests of the people. A justly famous line from the *Book of History* neatly captures this important point: "Heaven sees as the people see; heaven hears as the people hear." In doing the bidding of the people, heaven is not a willful or arbitrary force. It does not bestow and withdraw its Mandate capriciously as it alone pleases.

It should be clear, then, that there is nothing "fated" about the Mandate. Rulers win it through virtuous and benevolent rule; they lose it by abandoning virtuous and benevolent rule. It is not a matter of heaven's whimsy. A poem in the *Book of Odes* warns the successors of King Wen, the illustrious founder of the Zhou, that retaining the Mandate or losing it is in their hands:

> The Mandate is not easy to keep;
> may it not end in your own persons.
> Display and make bright your good fame,
> and consider what heaven did to the Yin [i.e., the Shang].
> The doings of high heaven

have no sound, no smell.
Make King Wen your pattern,
and all the states will trust in you.

The message here is emphatic: be virtuous and the Mandate is
yours; abandon virtue and lose the Mandate. In the end, it is the
ruler's relationship with, and treatment of, his people that decides
the fate of the Mandate, not heaven. The Mandate of Heaven thus
stands in rather sharp contrast to the European doctrine of the
"divine right of kings," where rulers are granted the right to rule
directly from God and are accountable for their actions to God alone.
Not subject to the will of the people, their authority is absolute.

It was on the occasion of the Zhou conquest of the Shang in the
mid-eleventh century BCE that the principles of the Mandate of
Heaven were first articulated by the Duke of Zhou. If the theory of
the Mandate was brilliant propaganda—serving to legitimize the
Zhou conquest of the Shang—it could, nonetheless and just as
readily, serve to legitimize the conquest of the Zhou by others.
This is why poems in the *Odes* and documents in the *History*
implore the Zhou leaders to dedicate themselves to the cultivation
of virtue as the basis of their legitimacy. The Mandate is
precarious: it can be won, and it can be lost.

So ingrained would become this notion of the Mandate of Heaven
that when the foreign, "barbarian" Manchus entered the city of
Beijing in 1644 and proclaimed the establishment of the Qing
dynasty (1644–1912), the first edict the leaders issued, inviting the
Chinese populace to welcome Manchu rule, invoked the spirit and
language of the Mandate of Heaven:

The empire is not an individual's private property. Whosoever
possesses virtue holds it. The army and the people are not an
individual's property. Whosoever possesses virtue commands them.
We now occupy the empire.

Chapter 4

Variety within early Confucianism

In considering the success of the Confucian tradition, its ability to endure over the course of a couple of millennia—even into the twenty-first century—we must be mindful of this simple fact: Confucianism was ever changing. This is hardly surprising, as all major systems of belief are sustained by change and variety. Few, after all, would assume that the Christianity of Thomas Aquinas was the Christianity of St. Paul, or that the Christianity of Ignatius of Loyola was the Christianity of John Calvin. The different theological outlooks of these men, to be sure, all emerged from the general vision outlined in the Hebrew Bible and in the New Testament and thus share certain core beliefs. But at the same time, these thinkers from different ages and places naturally brought to their reflection on the foundational teachings a range of social and religious priorities, which resulted in "Christianities" with different, sometimes widely different, emphases. This ability of Christianity to keep itself relevant to different people and changing times and places is what has enabled it to survive and remain vital.

What is true of Christianity—and Judaism and Islam as well—is equally true of Confucianism. Yet in much of the West, until the early years of the twentieth century, Confucianism was regarded as some sort of unchanging monolith, a stagnant tradition that had undergone little change since the time of its founder and was responsible for China's "backwardness" in the nineteenth and twentieth centuries. Whether this view was born of ignorance of the Confucian tradition or of Western self-satisfaction with its version of material progress in these same centuries, it has since given way in the twentieth and twenty-first centuries to a much richer understanding of the vibrancy of Confucianism in the history of East Asia generally and of China in particular.

The vision outlined by Confucius lent itself to a variety of interpretations. These interpretations, though anchored in a set of shared foundational beliefs, could nonetheless evolve, as did Christianity, into quite distinctive "Confucianisms." Students of China speak of classical Confucianism, Mencian Confucianism, the Confucianism of Xunzi, Han Confucianism, Song Confucianism, Neo-Confucianism, utilitarian Confucianism, Wang Yangming Confucianism, and so on. The reader need not fear: I have no interest in cataloguing all the various schools within Confucianism here or elaborating on their major differences. My aim is simply to show how the Master's vision could unfold differently in the hands of different interpreters. The focus will be on his most prominent earlier followers—Mencius (fourth c. BCE) and Xunzi (third c. BCE)—whose "competing" interpretations of Confucius's vision would endure throughout imperial Chinese history. (Chapter 5 will treat the influential "Neo-Confucian" reinterpretation of Confucianism—the standard interpretation of Confucian teachings in the later imperial period.)

We do not have precise dates for either Mencius or Xunzi, but we can comfortably place Mencius in the heart of the fourth century BCE and Xunzi in the very late fourth but mostly third century BCE. Mencius hailed from the small state of Zou in northeast China. From Zou, he set out to find a ruler sympathetic to his views and, as the text in his name indicates, had audiences with a few of them. But he failed to gain the sympathetic ear he had hoped and thus, like Confucius before him, turned to teaching. The text of the *Mencius*, in seven "books," is said to be a record of conversations compiled by disciples between Mencius and rulers of the day, his disciples, and philosophical interlocutors.

Xunzi was a native of Zhao in the central part of north China. He spent much of his later life as an academician of the Jixia Academy, a center of lively intellectual debate at the court of Qi in northeast China. His eponymous text, the *Xunzi*, in thirty-two chapters or sections, is different from both the *Analects* and the *Mencius*: it is not a record of conversations or aphorisms but a set of self-contained essays thought to be written by Xunzi himself. Hence what we find in the *Xunzi* is sustained argumentation, a text far less fragmentary in composition than either the *Analects* or the *Mencius*.

Both Mencius and Xunzi fully embraced the Master's core beliefs: (1) that man can become a sage; (2) that moral goodness results from self-cultivation; (3) that learning is a part of the self-cultivation process; (4) that a vanguard elite is essential in promoting morality among the people; and (5) that good governance depends on the virtue of the ruler, who creates the right conditions whereby the people can become good and society can become harmonious.

Yet there were fundamental disagreements between the two great thinkers, most especially over the source of man's moral perfectibility. Mencius locates that source internally in human nature, asserting that man is born with a nature that naturally tends toward goodness, just as water naturally tends to flow downhill (6A.2). Man must learn to develop this innate goodness—in the face of external forces that might lead him astray—in order to achieve moral perfection. Xunzi strongly objects, unambiguously proclaiming: "Man's nature is evil" (sec. 23, "Man's Nature is Evil"). To find the moral resources that will enable him to redirect his recalcitrant human nature, man needs to look externally, to his environment and culture. With such starkly different assumptions about man's inherent

50

nature—and consequently about where the source of man's morality is to be found—it is unsurprising that the particular paths Mencius and Xunzi propose for achieving moral perfection diverge as well, especially in the important areas of self-cultivation and learning.

Mencius

1. On human nature and self-cultivation

In stating that human nature is good just as water flows downhill, Mencius is not arguing that all men *are* good—but rather that by the nature endowed in them they are all *inclined toward goodness*. Not everyone actualizes this goodness, just as water does not *always* flow downhill (consider, Mencius says, water that has been dammed or forced uphill). The goodness of human nature is an inherent potential that must be developed or nurtured. As Mencius explains, goodness in human nature is like shoots that must be given the opportunity to grow:

> All people have a mind-and-heart that cannot bear to see the suffering of others.... Here is why I say that all men have a mind-and-heart that cannot bear to see the suffering of others: today, no matter the person, if he suddenly comes upon a young child about to fall into a well, his mind-and-heart fills with alarm and is moved to compassion. It is not because he wishes to ingratiate himself with the parents of the young child; nor is it because he seeks renown among villagers and friends; nor is it because he would hate the bad reputation. From this we can see that to be without a mind-and-heart of compassion is not to be human; to be without a mind-and-heart that is ashamed of evil in oneself and hates it in others is not to be human; to be without a mind-and-heart of humility and deference is not to be human; to be without a mind-and-heart of right and wrong is not to be human. The mind-and-heart of compassion is the shoot of true goodness (*ren*); the mind-and-heart that is ashamed of evil in oneself and hates it in others is the shoot of righteousness; the mind-and-heart

of humility and deference is the shoot of ritual propriety; the mind-and-heart of right and wrong is the shoot of wisdom. People have these four shoots just as they have the four limbs.... All of us have these four shoots within us; if we know to develop and bring each to completion, it will be like a blaze catching fire or a spring finding a path. He who is able to bring them to completion is capable of preserving all within the four seas; he who doesn't complete them is incapable of caring for his parents. (2A.6)

For Mencius, each and every human being is born with the four shoots of true goodness, righteousness, ritual propriety, and wisdom. To be without these shoots "is not to be human"; they are no less a part of man's normal, natural make-up than are man's four limbs. To persuade us of the rightness of his belief he asks us, his readers, to imagine encountering a young, defenseless child about to fall into a well. That every one of us, he argues, would *instinctively* be moved to compassion is evidence that the shoot of compassion is within each of us.

The astute reader may have noticed, however, that nowhere in this passage does Mencius go on to say that having been moved to compassion, we would *all* actually rush to rescue the child. This is not mere oversight on Mencius's part. It is essential to his philosophical position and speaks to his belief that there exists a gap between the "four shoots" endowed in us at birth and their maturation into true goodness, righteousness, ritual propriety, and wisdom. There are some who, when they encounter the child facing almost certain death, may pause to assess, "Will I benefit from rescuing the child?" "Will I suffer injury in the rescue process?" or "Will I be held liable for the child's death?" These people, Mencius asserts, are no different in their human nature from other people; they too possess the shoots of true goodness, righteousness, ritual propriety, and wisdom. But, unlike those who rush to save the child without calculation or concern for their safety, their shoots of morality have not been nurtured to maturity. This is where self-cultivation plays an essential role.

To illustrate what happens if man's moral shoots are left uncultivated, Mencius tells the story of Ox Mountain. In this story, Mencius also suggests—without being as explicit as we might like—that the source of man's evil is the back-and-forth of everyday life. His daily needs for sustenance and his competition with others for limited resources put him at great risk of losing hold of his innate goodness:

> The trees on Ox Mountain were once quite luxuriant. But as they were just on the outskirts of the capital, axes chopped them down one by one. Could they remain luxuriant? And yet, given the renewal that goes on day and night and the nourishment that rain and dew bring, shoots and buds never fail to sprout. But then cattle and sheep come to graze. This is what accounts for the bald appearance of the mountain. When people see its baldness, they assume it was never wooded. But could this really be the nature of the mountain?
>
> The same is true of what belongs to a person: can he really be without the mind-and-heart of true goodness and righteousness? His letting go of his originally good mind-and-heart is like the axe chopping down the trees: if day after day it is chopped away, can it remain luxuriant? And yet, given the renewal that goes on day and night and the restorative vital energy that accompanies the dawn, his likes and dislikes will still bear some small resemblance to those of other people. But what he does during the day will fetter and destroy it [the originally good mind-and-heart] completely. If it is fettered repeatedly, the restorative vital energy of the nighttime will be insufficient to sustain it. And if the restorative vital energy of the nighttime is insufficient to sustain it, he will become little different from a beast. When others see a beast, they will assume that it never had a natural disposition for goodness. But could this really be the natural tendency of the man? Thus if it receives nourishment, there is nothing that will not grow; if it does not receive nourishment, there is nothing that will not decay. Confucius said, "Hold on to it and you preserve it; let go of it and you lose it…." Isn't it of the mind-and-heart that he speaks? (6A.8)

This passage underscores the point that all human beings, no matter how depraved-seeming, are born with precisely the same good human nature. Even a serial killer is so endowed, though simply by looking at him we would hardly know it. Just as the constant lopping of trees by axmen and the eating of young shoots and buds by sheep and cattle rob Ox Mountain of any semblance of its natural vegetation, forces external to a man's nature can cut down his shoots of morality and rob him of any semblance of humanity. This is why "holding on" to the original mind-and-heart is so urgent; for it is here, in this mind-and-heart, that the four shoots of virtue are located.

Holding on to the mind-and-heart is thus what distinguishes the morally superior man from others. It is this mind-and-heart, Mencius says, that enables man to think and reflect; and only by thinking and reflecting is man capable of keeping to the right path—of warding off the perils and lures of the external world—thereby giving his four inborn shoots of true goodness, righteousness, ritual propriety, and wisdom the opportunity to grow to maturity—to develop fully. It is such growth that results in man's moral perfection.

2. On the ruler

It is the explicit responsibility of the ruler, Mencius argues, to assist his subjects in their efforts to keep to the right path. To this end, the ruler is enjoined, in what is an especially eloquent passage in the text, to provide for the material well-being of his people:

> If the people lack a constant livelihood it follows that they will lack a constant mind-and-heart. And if they lack a constant mind-and-heart, they will become reckless and depraved, and there is nothing they will not do. To lead them into crime and then follow it up with punishment is to entrap the people. Is it possible that a truly good man in a high position would entrap the people? For this reason, an enlightened ruler supervises the livelihood of the people, making sure that they can adequately serve their parents above and children

below, and that in good years they are abundantly full and in bad years escape death. Only afterward does he urge them on toward goodness (*shan*, 善); in this way, the people will find it easy to follow him. (1A.7)

Confucius, too, had suggested that only when their basic material needs have been satisfied will the people be susceptible to moral instruction. But Mencius goes on at much greater length, proposing specific and concrete measures that a good ruler should take in promoting the people's well-being:

Do not interfere with the farming seasons, and the crops will be more than can be consumed; do not let finely meshed nets be cast in ponds and lakes, and the fish and turtles will be more than can be consumed; let axes enter the mountain groves only at the appropriate time, and the timber will be more than can be used. When crops and fish and turtles are more than can be consumed, and timber is more than can be used, the people will nurture the living and mourn the dead in contentment. Their nurturing of the living and the mourning of the dead in contentment: such is the beginning of the kingly way. Let mulberry trees be planted in households of five *mu*, and fifty-year olds can wear silk; do not let the times for breeding chickens, pigs, dogs, and hogs be neglected, and the seventy-year olds can eat meat. In fields of one hundred *mu*, do not deprive them of the seasons, and families of several mouths will never go hungry. Be attentive to instruction in the village schools and set forth the principles of filial piety and fraternal respect, and those with graying hair will not be on the roads carrying heavy loads on their.backs and heads. It is impossible in a state where seventy-year olds wear silk and eat meat, and the black-haired people suffer from neither hunger nor cold, for the ruler not to be regarded as a true king. If pigs and hogs eat the food meant for the people and you know not how to restrain them, and if there are famished dying on the roads and you know not how to distribute aid from the granaries, and then say, "It is not me, it is just a bad year," how is this any different from mutilating and killing a person and then saying, "it is not me, it is the weaponry." Let the king not put blame on a bad harvest, and all under heaven will come to him. (1A.3; cf. 1A.5 and 1A.7)

Such are the policies and practices of a "true king."

Mencius criticizes the rulers of his day, claiming that they are concerned more with profit and wealth for themselves than with the welfare of their people. The very first passage of his text conveys Mencius's displeasure with King Hui of Liang:

> Mencius went to see King Hui of Liang. The king said, "Sir. You've come here from a very great distance. Surely you've brought something that will be of profit to my state?" Mencius responded, "Why must Your Majesty use the word 'profit'? Surely, it is true goodness and righteousness alone that matter. If the king were to say, 'what will be of profit to my state?' and the high officials were to say, 'what will be of profit to my family?' and gentlemen and commoners were to say, 'what will be of profit to myself?' then everyone above and below would turn to attacking one another for profit, and the state thereby would be put in grave danger.... Let Your Majesty say, 'It is true goodness and righteousness alone that matter.' Why must Your Majesty use the word 'profit'?" (1A.1)

A ruler who speaks of profit prompts his people as well to speak of—and pursue—profit, which not only leads them astray, away from attending to their moral shoots, but ironically does nothing to profit the ruler or his state. The ruler's job, as Confucius stated earlier, is to be a moral exemplar: "When the prince is truly good, everyone else is truly good; when the prince is righteous, everyone else is truly righteous" (4B.5). In short, for Mencius, good government is one that provides food and shelter and sets a moral example for the people, thereby creating an environment, material and moral, in which the innate sprouts of true goodness, righteousness, ritual propriety, and wisdom can grow naturally and without impediment.

Mencius goes so far as to assert that only a ruler who practices this sort of benevolent government, who places the people first (7B.14), is a true ruler. According to tradition, Jie, the last king of the legendary Xia dynasty, and Zhou, the last king of the Shang dynasty, were cruel tyrants. Thus, when King Xuan of Qi asked,

> "Is it the case that Tang banished Jie and King Wu cut down Zhou?" Mencius responded, "So it says in the records." King Xuan said, "Is it permissible for a minister to murder his sovereign?" Mencius said, "A thief of true goodness is called 'thief'; a thief of righteousness is called 'criminal.' Thieves and criminals are called good-for-nothings. I have heard of the punishment of the good-for-nothing Zhou; I have not heard of the murder of a sovereign." (1B.8)

In arguing that a sovereign is to be called a sovereign only when he comports himself as a "true" sovereign should, Mencius is associating himself with his Master's call for the "rectification of names": the belief that names and reality must be brought into perfect accord (*Analects* 13.3). Killing Zhou, in Mencius's judgment, is not a matter of regicide, but rather a matter of killing a good-for-nothing who abandoned the proper way of a ruler and so abandoned being a real ruler. Mencius's point here, which will resonate powerfully throughout imperial Chinese history, is that a ruler who does not behave as a true sovereign, caring for the people with benevolence and righteousness, may be deposed.

While rulers may be deposed, there is no call here for popular revolution, as it is the ministers alone who have the right to depose an evil ruler (cf. 5B.9). Still, with this passage, the ruler's responsibility to care for the welfare of the people—to provide an environment where the people's shoots of virtue might develop—is backed up by a powerful sanction—the removal of the ruler by force. Over the centuries, this passage has sometimes been cited—though not entirely accurately, as I have indicated—as support for the right to popular rebellion.

Xunzi

1. On human nature and self-cultivation

On the question of human nature, our two philosophers could hardly be in more conspicuous disagreement. If for Mencius human nature contains the shoots of true goodness, for Xunzi it is the very source of man's immorality and waywardness. Taking direct aim at his predecessor, Xunzi declares, "Mencius states that man's nature is good (*shan*), but I say that this view is wrong" (sec. 23, "Man's Nature is Evil"). In the opening to a chapter devoted entirely to the proposition that "man's nature is evil," Xunzi explains:

> Man's nature is evil; goodness is the result of deliberate action. The nature of man is such that he is born with a fondness for profit. If he indulges this fondness, it will lead him into wrangling and strife, and all sense of courtesy and humility will disappear. He is born with feelings of envy and hate, and if he indulges these, they will lead him into violence and crime, and all sense of loyalty and good faith will disappear. Man is born with the desires of the eyes and ears, with the fondness for beautiful sights and sounds. If he indulges these, they will lead him into license and wantonness, and all ritual principles and correct forms will be lost. Hence, any man who follows his nature and indulges his emotions will inevitably become involved in wrangling and strife, will violate the forms and rules of society, and will end as a criminal. (sec. 23, "Man's Nature is Evil")

Xunzi insists that man has to turn away from his nature in order to become good. And so—like Mencius before him—he attaches great importance to the cultivation process. But for Xunzi the aim is not the nurturing of man's inborn nature; it is the restraint and redirecting of man's natural impulses.

Given his view of human nature and the need to "reform" it, Xunzi places considerably more emphasis on the role of learning and ritual principles in the cultivation process than does Mencius. Learning and rituals are essential tools in acculturating man, in reshaping his recalcitrant nature. For Mencius, who assumes human nature to be naturally inclined toward the good, these tools are simply less necessary. It is not that Mencius entirely dispenses with them, but they are not given the same prominence in his thinking that they are in Xunzi's, where gentle nurturing of the emergent shoots within is more essential.

The essential role that learning plays in Xunzi's variety of Confucianism is revealed in the very first passage of the *Xunzi* text:

> Learning should never cease. Blue comes from the indigo plant but is bluer than the plant itself. Ice is made of water but is colder than the water ever is. A piece of wood as straight as a plumb line may be bent into a circle as true as any drawn with a compass, and even after the wood has dried, it will not straighten out again. The bending process has made it that way. Thus if wood is pressed against a straightening board, it can be made straight; if metal is put to the grindstone, it can be sharpened; and if the gentleman studies widely and each day examines himself, his wisdom will become clear and his conduct without fault. (sec. 1, "Encouraging Learning")

Learning is endowed here with the enormous power to take the raw, unruly, and selfish stuff of man's nature and mold—indeed, *force*—it into morally sensitive tissue.

As we have seen, Mencius, by contrast, does not view learning as the forceful reshaping tool it is for Xunzi for the simple reason that for him man's moral "shoots" need but gentle cultivation, not an aggressive bending, dying, or grinding, to produce true goodness. Thus, while Mencius may encourage man to "learn widely" (4B.15), as Confucius did (e.g., 6.27, 9.2), and may urge true kings to establish schools for illuminating proper social relations, as rulers during the glorious Three Dynasties did (3A.3), learning in the sense of disciplined study or schooling does not hold the urgency for him that it does for Xunzi and consequently receives far less systematic attention from him.

If, for Xunzi, learning is to be an effective tool of transformation, it has to be the *right* learning. For this reason he lays out a model curriculum, one to be followed throughout a lifetime:

> Where does learning begin, and where does it end? I say that as to program, learning begins with the recitation of the Classics and ends with the reading of the ritual texts; and as to objective, it begins with learning to be a man of breeding and ends with learning to be a sage. If you truly pile up effort, you will enter into the highest realm. Learning continues until death, and only then does it cease. Therefore, we may speak of an end to the program of learning, but the objective of learning must never for an instant be given up. To pursue it is to be a man, to give it up is to become a beast. (sec. 1, "Encouraging Learning")

Xunzi offers further curricular direction, prescribing the subjects and the "textbooks" to be covered—and even suggesting the sequence in which they should be taken up:

> The *Book of History* is the record of government affairs, the *Book of Poetry* the repository of correct sounds, and the rituals are the great basis of law and the foundation of precedents. Therefore, learning reaches its completion with the rituals, for they may be said to represent the highest point of the Way and its power. The reverence and order of the rituals, the fitness and harmony of music, the breadth of the *Poetry* and the *History*, the subtlety of the *Spring and Autumn Annals*—these encompass all that is between heaven and earth. (sec. 1, "Encouraging Learning")

This passage represents the earliest effort in the long Confucian tradition to establish a coherent curriculum for students of the Way.

Rituals, as should be evident, are at the heart of Xunzi's learning program. It is through the guidance of ritual, Xunzi argues, that man's proclivity for evil can be restrained and that, over time, his behavior can become habituated to doing good:

> A straight piece of wood does not have to wait for the straightening board to become straight; it is straight by nature. But a warped piece of wood must wait until it has been laid against the straightening board, steamed and forced into shape before it can become straight, because by nature it is warped. Similarly since man's nature is evil, he must wait for the ordering power of the sage kings and the transforming power of ritual principles; only then can he achieve order and conform to goodness. (sec. 23, "Man's Nature is Evil")

Xunzi ends this passage with what is a refrain throughout his writings—the purposeful, mindful effort to reform or redirect our unruly inborn nature: "From this it is obvious, then, that man's nature is evil, and that his goodness is the result of deliberate action."

For Mencius, as we might expect, ritual does not have the same "straightening" or restraining effect since restraint is not called for in his view of the innate goodness of human nature. In Mencius's understanding, correct ritual practice—like true goodness, righteousness, and wisdom—is but the natural realization of man's good nature; it is, in his words, an "adornment" of true goodness and righteousness (4A.27; cf. 7A.21), not an instrument for producing these virtues.

For Xunzi, though, rituals are an essential part of self-cultivation. They do, as he explains in the passage cited above, serve to "straighten," but they also nurture man emotionally and psychologically. Proper ritual practice allows man to give expression to his emotions without risk of disrupting the social order. By moderating or "civilizing" his unruly innate emotions and desires, rituals enable man to harmonize his affective world with the larger world around him: "Rituals trim what is too long and stretch out what is too short, eliminate excess and remedy deficiency, extend the forms of love and reverence, and step-by-step bring to completion the beauty of proper conduct" (sec. 19, "A Discussion of Rites"). Ritual thus makes possible man's emotional fulfillment, even while it restrains his most anarchic emotional impulses. Xunzi remarks, "All rituals begin in simplicity, are brought to fulfillment in elegant form, and end in joy. When rituals are performed in the highest manner, then both the emotions and the forms embodying them are fully realized" (sec. 19, "A Discussion of Rites"). Performed well, then, ritual has a powerful beauty, an aesthetic appeal that uplifts man and contributes to his emotional well-being.

Finally, ritual also serves the important function of demarcating the various statuses in society—a function Confucius himself would surely have endorsed. Xunzi comments:

> Where ranks are all equal, there will not be enough goods to go around; where power is equally distributed, there will be a lack of unity; where there is equality among the masses, it will be impossible to employ them.... If men are of equal power and station and have the same likes and dislikes, then there will not be enough goods to supply their wants, and they will inevitably quarrel. Quarrelling must lead to disorder and disorder to exhaustion. The former kings abhorred such disorder, and therefore they regulated the principles of ritual in order to set up ranks. (sec. 9, "The Regulations of a King")

Rituals reinforce the hierarchy of society. They lend cohesion and stability to that hierarchy, encouraging all—"rich and poor," "eminent and humble"—to play their roles as they should.

2. The mind and moral perfectibility

We should not let Xunzi's rather dark view of human nature obscure an essential point: he believes as fervently as Mencius does in the moral perfectibility of men. He writes:

> The man in the street can become a Yu [the sage king]…. Any man in the street has the essential faculties needed to understand true goodness, righteousness, and proper standards, and the potential ability to put them into practice. Therefore, it is clear that he can become a Yu. (sec. 23, "Man's Nature is Evil")

It is, in short, because man is born with a faculty for knowing, for discriminating right from wrong, that he is able to come to understand morality from his environment. If in Mencius it is man's nature that distinguishes him most starkly from beasts, in Xunzi it is man's capacity to know and to put into practice what he knows, through conscious activity, that separates him most clearly from other creatures.

But while man may be capable of understanding morality, why should he want to? Why would man, born evil with "natural" selfish desires, love of profit, and feelings of envy and hate, have any impulse to turn toward the good? In other words, why would he of evil nature choose to submit to the straightening tools of learning and ritual in the first place? Xunzi's explanation is fascinating:

> Every man who desires to do good does so precisely because his nature is evil. A man whose accomplishments are meager longs for greatness; an ugly man longs for beauty; a man in cramped quarters longs for spaciousness; a poor man longs for wealth; a humble man longs for eminence. Whatever a man lacks in himself he will seek outside. But if a man is already rich, he will not long for wealth, and if he is already eminent, he will not long for greater power. What a man already possesses in himself he will not bother to look for

outside. From this we can see that men desire to do good precisely because their nature is evil. (sec. 23, "Man's Nature is Evil")

It is expressly because of the selfish desires and feelings of envy and jealousy with which we are born that we aggressively seek to possess the goodness we do not yet have. Here man does not pursue goodness for the sake of goodness, at least initially, but rather to satisfy his longing for what is not his. The pursuit of morality, ironically, is thus born of selfishness and avarice.

But it is not man's selfish nature alone that explains his impulse to seek out good. It is also the mind's realization that if he gives free expression to his unruly inborn tendencies, "chaos and mutual destruction" result (sec. 23, "Man's Nature is Evil"). Concluding that chaos and mutual destruction are not in his self-interest, that they do not ultimately enable him to satisfy his desires, the mind looks to restrain his innate tendencies and turns to ritual principles and classical teachings for guidance.

3. On the ruler

The responsibility of the ruler, according to Xunzi, is to establish order among people innately averse to it. The ruler understands that the people's inborn passions and desires must be restrained if social order and harmony are to be achieved. Through routine ritual instruction, he ventures to curb these passions and desires, and thus acculturate the people to a pattern of socially appropriate behavior.

Xunzi recognizes, however, that there are some subjects for whom the relatively gentle force of ritual will be insufficient, men whose impulses are so unruly that other, more assertive means of control are required. For this reason, he argues that the ruler should also employ law and punishment as means of keeping order. Xunzi's ideal is a society in which order and harmony are created and maintained largely through the transformative influence of ritual practice; when ritual fails, however, the ruler must rely on the more coercive instruments of law and punishment.

This ideal society can be realized only under a "true king." It is the good and righteous ruler alone who is capable of taking the true measure of his people and of determining how best to suppress their self-interest. He is a keen and fair judge, knowing unerringly when to guide by ritual and when to compel through law and punishment. Because he is caring and kind in his treatment of them, the people willingly lend him their support.

Xunzi is quite realistic in his assessment of the likelihood that a "true king" would actually come to power in his own day. Unlike Mencius, who spends much of his life trying to persuade contemporary rulers to strive to become true kings, Xunzi acknowledges that perhaps the best that could be hoped for is a ruler capable of imposing order—whether it be through law and punishment or military might—on his state. The age of the sage rulers, he concludes, is long past; needed now is a hegemon or strongman (*ba*, 霸) who can at least ensure a stable government and an ordered social hierarchy, if not a population morally perfected and harmonized through ritual.

Man and heaven in Mencius and Xunzi

In the fourth century BCE Mencius argues that heaven is an ethical entity. A short century later, Xunzi characterizes heaven as a naturalistic entity, operating according to its own internal rhythms and without any ethical impulses; heaven, for him, approximates "nature" or the "natural order." Given these different views, it is quite natural that the two philosophers understand the role that heaven plays in the life of man differently as well.

A close ethical connection exists between man and heaven, according to Mencius:

There are honors bestowed by heaven, and there are honors
bestowed by man. True goodness, righteousness, conscientiousness,
trustworthiness, unflagging delight in the good—these are honors
bestowed by heaven. (6A.16)

Heaven is responsible for what is moral in man. For it is from
heaven that man receives his shoots of virtue. If he is to become
fully good, fully human, it is his obligation to develop these shoots.
By developing them, he is conforming with—and satisfying—
heaven's ethical plan for him. In a sense, then, heaven is dictating,
biologically, man's norms of behavior.

In a passage in the *Mencius* that is rather unique in its cosmic
scope and suggestion of cosmic unity, the philosopher states:

> For a man to give full realization to his mind-and-heart is for him to
> understand his own nature, and a man who knows his own nature will
> know heaven. The retention of his mind-and-heart and the nurturing
> of his nature are the means by which he serves heaven. (7A.1)

Mencius means here to impress on his followers the binding
ethical connectedness between man and heaven. If heaven is the
author of man's morality, of the moral potential embedded in
man's mind-and-heart, the realization of this morality yields
insight into heaven's design. This is to know heaven. Fulfilling the
task heaven imposes on us at birth, carrying out the ethical
responsibilities it seeds in us, is to serve heaven. The term "serve"
reminds us too that ultimately we are subordinate to the morally
legislative force of heaven.

Xunzi's understanding of heaven could hardly be more different.
For him, heaven is naturalistic, without intent, and thus has no
ethical connection to humankind. In fact, Xunzi is highly critical
of the widespread contemporary belief that heaven communicates
with man, signaling its approval and disapproval of him through
omens and portents:

> When stars fall or trees make strange sounds, all people in the
> country are terrified and go about asking, "Why has this happened?"
> For no special reason, I reply. It is simply that, with the changes of
> heaven and earth and the mutations of the *yin* and *yang*, such
> things once in a while occur. You may wonder at them, but you
> must not fear them. (sec. 17, "A Discussion of Heaven")

Heaven here is the natural order. Its manifestations are nothing
but the spontaneous "mutations of the *yin* and *yang*" of the
universe. This is not an interested or willful heaven
"communicating" with or responding to human activity. Xunzi's
writings are insistent in their rebuke of those who believe that
heaven is an entity responsive to their entreaties: "You pray for
rain and it rains. Why? For no particular reason, I say. It is just as
though you had not prayed for rain and it rained anyway." And, he
reminds them, "heaven does not suspend the winter because men
dislike the cold" (sec. 17, "A Discussion of Heaven"). His insistence
indicates how pervasive he regards the "superstitious" practices
and beliefs of the day to be. And the message he hopes to convey is
emphatic: Heaven is unconcerned with man!

It is because there is no ethically connected or concerned heaven
that human beings must look to the sages and the rituals they
created for moral guidance. Heaven offers no moral endowment,
no moral assistance. Indeed, in Xunzi's view, what made the sages
of the past—Yao, Shun, and Yu—deserving of reverence and praise
is that they alone grasped that man requires a set of ritual
principles and teachings to give him moral direction.

When all goes well for man, when all goes well for society, it is
entirely man's doing. Man must come to realize that his lot is not a
matter of heaven's will or fate, as many would believe:

> Are order and disorder due to heaven? I reply, the sun and the
> moon, the stars and the constellations, revolved in the same way in
> the time of Yu as in the time of Jie. Yu achieved order; Jie brought

disorder. Hence order and disorder are not due to heaven. (sec. 17, "A Discussion of Heaven")

Man's lot depends simply on man's efforts.

Although heaven does not exist for the purpose of providing for man, Xunzi acknowledges that in its "mutations of *yin* and *yang*," heaven does have powerful effects on man. Xunzi exhorts man to be alert to these effects and to make the best possible use of them.

> Is it better to exalt heaven and contemplate it,
> Or to nourish its creatures and regulate them?
> Is it better to follow heaven and sing hymns to it,
> Or to take hold of what heaven mandates and make use of it?
> Is it better to look ahead to the seasons and await what they bring,
> Or respond to the seasons and exploit them?
> Is it better to wait for things to increase of themselves,
> Or to develop their capacities and transform them? (sec. 17,
>   "A Discussion of Heaven")

For Xunzi, heaven is separate and other, without interest in the human world or in man's well-being; yet through the conscious effort described here, man can find in the effects of heaven's ever-mutating *yin* and *yang*, in its constancy of change, much that benefits human life.

To conclude: Mencius and Xunzi, the founders of the two major branches of early Confucianism, agree: (1) that man is morally perfectible; and (2) that to achieve moral perfection man must undertake a self-cultivation process. But for Mencius, the source of man's moral potential is internal, found in man's nature itself; for Xunzi, it is to be found externally, in the culture, especially in the body of ritual created by the sages of antiquity. For Mencius, consequently, self-cultivation is largely a process of gentle nurturing, of keeping the growing inner goodness shielded from the harmful and corrupting influences of society; for Xunzi, the process is necessarily more expansive and aggressive, and looks directly to society for tools capable of "straightening" or reshaping man's inborn twisted nature. For Mencius, the ideal ruler is responsible for creating the right environment—moral and material—for his subjects, one in which man's moral potential can develop naturally and without impediment; for Xunzi, the ruler is more of a presence, actively guiding the behavior of his subjects and acquainting them with an array of cultural tools—ritual, law, punishment—necessary to curb their reckless impulses and become accustomed to a goodness foreign to their nature.

Xunzi's faith in the transformative power of learning and ritual has had an indelible influence on education and social practices throughout Chinese history. But Mencius's influence has been greater still: thinkers responsible for the grand reformulation of the Confucian intellectual tradition a millennium later would reject Xunzi's view of human nature and embrace Mencius's sunnier outlook that man is born with the shoots of perfect goodness within him.

Chapter 5

The reorientation of the Confucian tradition after 1000 CE: The teachings of Neo-Confucianism

Confucius, Mencius, and Xunzi would set the philosophical course for the Confucian tradition for more than the next one thousand years. But in the eleventh century there emerged a coterie of Confucian thinkers who began to rethink the teachings of their classical predecessors. Their "school" of Confucianism, known as *daoxue* (道學) or "Learning of the Way," and often referred to as Neo-Confucianism, would quickly come to dominate Chinese intellectual and political life. Indeed, by the thirteenth century, it had become the state orthodoxy—the statement of principles that ostensibly guided the Chinese imperial government and the foundation of the civil service examination systems—a status it would retain until the early years of the twentieth century.

Neo-Confucianism represents a reworking of the Confucian tradition. It upholds the values and ethics of classical Confucianism but reorients that Confucianism in two important ways: (1) it grounds the values and ethics of classical Confucianism in an elaborate system of metaphysics (that is, an explanation of the nature of being and knowing) generated over the eleventh and twelfth centuries; and (2) on the basis of this system of metaphysics, it creates a structured program of self-cultivation, a step-by-step template for "becoming a sage."

Why the emergence of Neo-Confucianism at this particular time? Looking around, Confucian scholar-officials of the Song period (960–1279) perceived their world to be in a state of crisis—politically, intellectually, and morally. Since the beginning of the dynasty in the tenth century, parts of the north China plain, the heartland of Chinese civilization, had been occupied by a string of non-Chinese tribes; in 1127 the last of these tribes, the Jurchen, captured the Song capital of Kaifeng and set up the Jin dynasty (1115–1234), forcing the Song court to flee south. The loss of the north was a terrible shock to Chinese scholar-officials. For them, it represented far more than just a straightforward military or political defeat; it meant that the Way was in steep decline. Had the Chinese emperor and his ministers been behaving as virtuous Confucian rulers and ministers should, the Way would have prevailed, and the north would not have been vulnerable to "barbarian" attack. What led these men to stray from the Confucian path of moral cultivation and virtuous government?

Many blamed another, earlier "barbarian" intrusion: Buddhism. This foreign teaching, introduced to China from India in the first century CE, became increasingly popular after the sixth century. Its allure was such that Confucians plaintively acknowledged, "Be they adults or children, officials, farmers, or merchants, men or women, all have entered the Buddhist fold." Even many scholars, the very men who were supposed to keep the Confucian Way alive and well, had been drawn to Buddhism over the years (especially to elite schools like Chan, more commonly known as Zen in the West), attracted by its philosophical exploration of human nature, the mind, ways of knowing, self-realization, and man's relation to the cosmos. Confucians viewed this popularity with dismay, fearful that Buddhism's preoccupation with the enlightenment of the individual was distracting people at all levels of society from their fundamental Chinese—and Confucian—obligation to better themselves morally for the purpose of serving society and promoting the welfare of others.

Beginning in the tenth and eleventh centuries, scholars who identified with the Confucian tradition, mindful of the challenges posed to the prominence of the Confucian Way, were given to deep reflection on how the challenges to their Way could be met. They turned to the canon of classical texts with an almost religious vigor, seeking in them those teachings—those truths—that would speak eloquently to the urgent issues of the day and thereby serve to resuscitate a Way in decline. Many men were involved in this tenth- and eleventh-century engagement with the canon, searching for its contemporary relevance. Among the most predominant of these thinkers were Zhou Dunyi (周敦頤) (1017–73), Zhang Zai (張載) (1020–77), Cheng Hao (程灝) (1032–85), and Cheng Yi (程頤) (1033–1107).

But this Song reflection on the meaning of the Confucian tradition would find its most influential voice in the next century with Zhu Xi (朱熹) (1130–1200), the great synthesizer of Song Neo-Confucianism. Based on the writings of these earlier Song thinkers, Zhu Xi's synthesis is given its full expression in a series of brilliant interlinear commentaries on the Confucian Classics. Zhu's genius rests on his presentation of a "new" Confucian philosophy that looks to and is justified by readings of what by his day were ancient—indeed archaic—texts. Deeply influenced by the ideas of his Song forerunners (and no doubt, too, by some of the concerns introduced and popularized by Buddhism), he constructs from the Classics, in the metaphysical language of his day, a systematic process of self-realization that, if followed scrupulously, was to lead the individual to sagehood. In true Confucian fashion, this morally perfected man—unlike the enlightened Buddhist—is fully committed to serving society and bringing harmony to the people. Through his efforts, and those of others like him, the once-great Way can be resuscitated.

Zhu Xi's Neo-Confucian metaphysics

The classical Confucian thinkers, Mencius and Xunzi, assume—albeit on different grounds—that man is capable of moral perfection. Zhu Xi, too, assumes that man is morally perfectible, but he develops a metaphysics that supports this assumption in new philosophical terms—or, rather, in old terms that he invests with new meanings. He embraces and provides ontological support for Mencius's belief that human nature is good, that all men are born with the beginnings of the four cardinal virtues: true goodness, righteousness, ritual propriety, and wisdom. Indeed, it is with Zhu Xi that the Mencian view of human nature triumphs over Xunzi's and becomes orthodox. But Zhu goes further to address the philosophical question left largely unresolved by Mencius: If men are born good, where and how does evil arise? And, having pinpointed the source of human evil, Zhu Xi then lays out a detailed, step-by-step program for eradicating evil and nurturing man's innate goodness.

The entire universe, Zhu Xi claims, is made up of *qi* (氣), translated variously as material force, matter-energy, vital energy, and psychophysical stuff (but in this volume will simply be left transliterated as *qi*). This *qi* is dynamic, circulating endlessly, coalescing in particular configurations to constitute particular things in the cosmos. However different the forms or shapes of things might be, they are all constituted of *qi*. In the words of his predecessor Zhang Zai:

> *Qi* moves and flows in all directions and in all manners. Its two elements [the primal forces of *yin* and *yang*] unite and give rise to the concrete. Thus the manifold diversity of human beings and things is produced. Through the ceaseless succession of these two elements of *yin* and *yang* the great meaning of the universe is established.

Qi is thus what binds everything in the universe together. This assumption of a shared, pervading cosmic *qi* has strong ethical implications for Zhu and his fellow Neo-Confucians. For if all things are constituted of *qi*, all things and people in the universe are interrelated. A well-known essay by Zhang Zai opens with the following lines:

> Heaven is my father, and earth is my mother, and even such a small creature as I finds an intimate place in their midst.
>
> Therefore that which extends throughout the universe I regard as my body and that which directs the universe I consider as my nature.
>
> All people are my brothers and sisters, and all things are my companions.

Related by a shared *qi*, people are to treat all other people as they would "brothers and sisters." This quasi-biological relationship among human beings helps to explain why, as Mencius suggested many centuries earlier, man spontaneously feels compassion toward others. Humankind, after all, is simply one big family.

This *qi* thus argues for the interconnectedness among all things in the universe, living and inanimate. But it is also this *qi* that accounts for the differences among the multitude of things. At birth different things receive different allotments of *qi*, varying in both quality and quantity. Human beings overall, Neo-Confucians explain, receive *qi* in its most clear and pure form, and it is precisely the quality of this *qi* that distinguishes them most sharply from other beings and things in the universe. Zhu's predecessor, Zhou Dunyi, writes:

> The interaction of the two *qi* [*yin* and *yang*] engenders and transforms the myriad things. The myriad things produce and reproduce, resulting in unending transformation. Human beings alone receive the most refined and spiritually efficacious *qi*.

He goes on to explain that it is because he is possessed of the "most refined and spiritually efficacious *qi*" that man, among all creatures, is singularly capable of moral discernment, or knowing the difference between good and evil. A tree receives the *qi* for a tree and consequently does not have a similar capability.

But *qi* is not the *source* of man's innate goodness. For just as all things in the universe are constituted of *qi*, all things are also possessed of *li* (理) or principle (sometimes translated "moral principle"). As Zhu Xi explains, "In the universe there has never been any *qi* without principle nor any principle without *qi*." If *qi* is what gives a thing its particular psychophysical form, the principle inhering in the thing is, in Zhu's words, "the reason why it is as it is and the rule to which it should conform." Every object, event, relationship, matter, and affair in the universe has principle. A boat has the attributes or normative properties of a boat, a cart the attributes of a cart, a tree the attributes of a tree, a human being the attributes of a human being, and the relationship between father and son the attributes of a relationship between father and son on account of principle. That man as a species is inherently good is owing to the principle inhering in man.

Thus principle is found in each and every thing and affair. Yet principle is ultimately one, Zhu insists. For him, the principle of the boat, the cart, the human being, the tree, and the father-son relationship is but a particular manifestation of the one universal principle. He frequently repeats the formula, "principle is one, its manifestations are many" (*li yi fen shu,* 理一分殊). "Principle," then, might best be understood as something like the underlying pattern or blueprint for the cosmos, encoded in each and every thing in the universe; the particular manifestation of principle designates the more particular role each thing is to play in the unified, cosmic plan. To rephrase Zhu's brief definition: each thing has its manifestation of principle, but the rule or pattern to which all things in the universe conform is ultimately one, as is the reason all things are as they are. Though without form or generative power, it is principle that provides coherence and order for a universe of ever-changing *qi*.

Following Mencius, Zhu Xi understood human nature to be precisely the same in each and every person, for each and every person is endowed at birth with the same four cardinal virtues. In wholeheartedly adopting the Mencian view of goodness of human nature, however, Zhu gives it a contemporary metaphysical grounding, arguing that human beings have the nature they have *because* human nature is identical with principle or *li* in man: "Human nature is simply this principle."

But if human nature is principle and thus always the same and always good, what accounts for "bad" people and "bad" behavior? Zhu Xi and his fellow Neo-Confucians look beyond Mencius (who never really answers this question satisfactorily) to elaborate an explanation of evil that is grounded in their understanding of *qi*. And what they conclude is that although man, relative to all other creatures in the universe, receives the highest-grade *qi,* each and every person receives a different allotment of *qi*; the quality and quantity of this allotment varies from one individual to another—in contrast to human nature, which is the same in everyone. Some *qi* is clearer than others, some more refined than others, and some less dense than others.

This allotment of *qi* gives each person his or her peculiar form and individual characteristics; it is what accounts for individuation among human beings. And it is this allotment of *qi* that, depending on its degree of clarity and density, either enables a person's innately good nature to shine forth or obscures it, preventing it from becoming manifest. Zhu Xi remarks to his disciples, "Human nature is principle. The reason that there are good and bad men is simply that each allotment of *qi* has its clarity and turbidity."

The particular endowment of *qi* that any individual receives at birth is fated. I happen to receive *this* quantity and quality of *qi,* and you happen to receive *that* quantity and quality of *qi.* But—and it is essential to understand this if we are to understand the Neo-Confucian project—our endowment of *qi* is malleable. It is because *qi* is dynamic and changeable, and because its change can be directed by human endeavor, that people can better themselves, even become sages. The clearest, most refined *qi*, if it is not properly tended to, can become turbid and coarse, but a turbid and coarse endowment can be nurtured into something more refined and clear. The challenge for each human being is to care for his allotment of *qi*, keeping or making it perfectly refined and clear so that the goodness, which is his nature, can reveal itself without obstruction.

This potential for perfection creates what is for Neo-Confucians *the* human moral predicament: man lives at all times with the capability to be fully moral and yet commonly finds himself falling short of moral perfection. He is possessed of an innate moral potential but a potential that must actively and consciously be given realization. To this end, his endowment of *qi* has to be nurtured, for it is the condition of his share of *qi* that determines whether his moral potential as a human being will be achieved. Zhu Xi thus shares with Mencius the view that man is perfectible; but by elaborating the meaning of the terms *li*, "principle," and *qi*, he and his fellow Neo-Confucians offer a detailed ontological explanation of *how* one can improve oneself.

Self-cultivation and the investigation of things

It is this moral predicament that explains the centrality of the self-cultivation process in the Neo-Confucian philosophical system. Self-cultivation is the conditioning process, the means by which the individual can refine his *qi*, thereby enabling the goodness that is in his human nature to be realized. In reflecting on the canon of texts in the Confucian tradition, Zhu Xi finds in the first chapter of the *Great Learning* (*Daxue*, 大學) what he regards as the basis of a Neo-Confucian program of self-cultivation for followers of the Confucian Way:

Those of antiquity...wishing to cultivate themselves, first set their
minds in the right; wishing to set their minds in the right, they first
made their intentions true; wishing to make their intentions true,
they first extended knowledge to the utmost; the extension of
knowledge lies in the investigation of things.

Self-cultivation thus rests on efforts to investigate things, a term
that had for many centuries been a matter of debate.

In a chapter of commentary that Zhu writes on this passage in the
Great Learning, he formulated what would become the orthodox
interpretation of "the extension of knowledge lies in the
investigation of things":

What is meant by "the extension of knowledge lies in the
investigation of things" is this: if we wish to extend our knowledge
to the utmost, we must probe thoroughly the principle in those
things that we encounter. Now every person's mind, with its
intelligence, is possessed of the capacity for knowing; at the same
time, every thing in the world is possessed of principle. To the
extent that principle is not thoroughly probed, a person's knowledge
is not fully realized. For this reason, the first step of instruction in
the *Great Learning* teaches students that, encountering anything at
all in the world, they must build on what they already know of
principle and probe still deeper, until they reach its limit. Exerting
themselves in this manner for a long time, they will one day
suddenly become all-penetrating; this being the case, the manifest
and the hidden, the subtle and obvious qualities of all things, will all
be known, and the mind, in its whole substance and vast operations,
will be completely illuminated. This is what is meant by "the
investigation of things." This is what is meant by "the completion
of knowledge."

The process proposed here is an inductive one. Man is required,
whenever he encounters any thing, any affair, or any relationship, to
look beyond its mere surface. He is to probe into and reflect on the

particular manifestation of principle that inheres in it, in order to get at its underlying truth. With time and effort, his understanding of things will deepen and broaden, resulting in an ever-clearer apprehension of the world around him. Probing principle thus begins with the particular but yields to an understanding of the universal principle that gives coherence to all things.

The aim of this investigation, of course, is not an understanding of the world for understanding's sake, nor is it scientific inquiry that is being proposed. Rather, if a person genuinely understands the true nature of things and affairs, if he truly recognizes why things, affairs, and relationships are as they are, he will be capable of dealing with those things, affairs, and relationships he encounters in the world in a perfectly appropriate way. Getting at the various manifestations of principle leads to an enlightened understanding of the cosmic order, which, in turn, results in moral awareness of how one ideally is to comport oneself with respect to all things and affairs in that cosmic order.

According to Zhu, what makes the apprehension of principle possible for each and every man is that we are all born, as Xunzi suggested, with a mind capable of understanding—an intelligence capable of penetrating the underlying principle in things. Yet, he acknowledges, not everyone achieves the sort of total illumination that is the goal of self-cultivation. For while the mind is capable of realizing principle and arriving at a cosmic understanding, it can also be led astray from such realization by excessive human emotions or creaturely desires. Hence, echoing the words of Mencius, Zhu Xi frequently admonishes disciples "to hold on to the mind" or "to seek the lost mind." As he says on one occasion, "It's simply because man has let go of his mind that he falls into evil." Or on another, "If a person is able to preserve his mind so that it is exceptionally clear, he'll naturally be capable of merging with the Way." For Zhu, the mind, which is constituted of only the most refined *qi*, is the "root." It must be tended to and kept refined if man is to behave as he should, in accord with principle.

Helping to guide the mind in the right direction is *zhi* (志), the will, which Zhu explains as the intention or the inclination of the mind or, literally, "where the mind is headed." Man must strive to keep this will firmly fixed; for if it is strong and determined, the will is sure to lead the mind along the right path toward apprehension of principle and away from insidious desires. *Lizhi* (立志), "to establish or fix the will," significantly, is one of Zhu Xi's most common refrains in his discussions with his disciples. Of course, the central importance of the will was suggested long before by the Master himself, when, in his "autobiographical" remark in the *Analects* (2.4), he related that fixing his will on learning at the age of fifteen had been the first step on his journey to moral perfection.

Zhu Xi's program of learning

As Zhu Xi explains, principle can be investigated anywhere and in anything. An individual could find principle looking at the natural world and its phenomena, at a filial son, at historical events and persons, at personal experiences and relationships. Principle inheres in all things and affairs, after all. But Zhu worries that such a broad and undefined field of inquiry will prove overwhelming and discourage individuals from taking up the investigation of things seriously. He wishes to provide students with more focused direction, suggesting what "things" in particular are likely to yield clear and direct apprehension of principle.

For Zhu Xi, these "things" turn out to be the texts of the ancient sages, the Confucian Classics: "All things in the world have principle, but its essence is embodied in the works of the sages and worthies. Hence, in seeking principle we must turn to these works." Because the Classics had been written by the great sages of antiquity—men who themselves had in their own lives come to refine their *qi* and apprehend principle fully—principle would be most clearly and readily manifest in them. There might be other ways to investigate principle, but studying the writings of the sages is simply the most efficient.

To give followers of the Confucian Way still further direction—in the hopes of making the Way as accessible as possible to them—Zhu Xi develops a coherent, sequential program of classical learning. From the canon, which by the late eleventh century has expanded to the Thirteen Classics from the original Five Classics, he selects four—referred to commonly after the thirteenth century as the Four Books—that he has students read before all others: the *Great Learning*, the *Analects*, the *Mencius*, and *Maintaining Perfect Balance*. The "ease, immediacy, and brevity" of these four works gives them an accessibility that other texts in the canon lack. They are the very foundation of all Confucian learning:

> In reading, begin with passages that are easy to understand.
> For example, principle is brilliantly clear in the *Great Learning*, *Maintaining Perfect Balance*, the *Analects*, and the *Mencius*—these four texts. Men simply do not read them. If these texts were understood, any book could be read, any principle could be investigated, any affair could be managed.

Only after mastering these four texts are students to turn to the so-called Five Classics, the texts that had been, for a millennium and a half since the Han period, the focal works of the tradition: the *Book of Changes*, the *Book of Poetry*, the *Book of History*, the *Book of Rites*, and the *Spring and Autumn Annals*.

The shift in emphasis advocated here by Zhu, away from the Five Classics and toward the Four Books, underscores an obvious point but one that should be made explicit: much as the Christian Bible offers a range of teachings that invite readers to take away a variety of meanings, so too does the Confucian canon of Thirteen Classics include multiple writings with different contents and emphases. The Five Classics and the Four Books may share a fundamental moral, social, and political vision, but the expression of that vision takes rather different forms in the two collections.

To generalize, the Five Classics illustrate Confucian morality using examples and lessons from ancient history; identify ideal institutions and methods of governance drawn from the past; describe in detail how one should conduct oneself in life's varying circumstances; and prescribe at length the ritualistic practices for maintaining a well-ordered society. From the Five Classics the ruler learns how to rule, the minister learns how to administer the realm, father and mother learn how to parent, children learn how to express filial devotion, older and younger learn how to show mutual respect, and friends learn how to be friends.

The Four Books tend to be less historical, descriptive, and concrete. Concerned primarily with the nature of man, the inner source of his morality, and his relation to the larger cosmos, they introduce and explain general principles of proper conduct and action and do not require the detailed, and often abstruse, knowledge of ancient Chinese institutions and social practices that comprehension of the Five Classics requires.

A shift from the Five Classics to the Four Books is something more than a curricular shift; it represents a major philosophical reorientation in the Confucian tradition "inward" toward teachings in the canon that place considerably more emphasis on the inner realm of human morality—and on the all-important process of self-cultivation. From the thirteenth century on, these Four Books—with Zhu's interlinear commentary on them—would make up the "core curriculum" in the Confucian tradition, the gateway to self-realization and true understanding.

Thus in Zhu's program of learning, there is a right set of texts to be read, and there is a right sequence in which to read them. But, just as importantly, there is a right *way* to read them. Over the course of many years, Zhu develops for his students an elaborate hermeneutics (or, to use his own term, *dushufa* [讀書法]), a comprehensive theory and method of reading the canonical texts. Merely passing one's eyes over a text will not produce genuine understanding, he warns. For the writings of the sages to reveal their truths, the reader must approach them with a seriousness of purpose, with the proper mental attitude. He is to be fully attentive, free of all other concerns and distractions: "In reading, you want both body and mind to enter into the passage. Don't concern yourself with what's going on elsewhere, and you'll see the principle in the passage." To this end, Zhu advocates the practice of quiet-sitting or meditation, for it settles and clears the reader's mind, leaving it perfectly open and receptive to the message of the sages.

The reader is expected to recite the classical text over and over again until he no longer sees it as "other." This repeated recitation results in memorization of the text, but the process is anything but mechanical or "rote"; each reading-and-recitation produces a deeper, more subtle and personal understanding of it. There is no prescribed number of times a text should be read, Zhu says, commenting only, "when the number's sufficient, stop," but he acknowledges that in some instances fifty or a hundred readings may not be too many. Zhu Xi's hermeneutical goal is straightforward: the follower of the Way, through recitation and memorization of the Classics, is to internalize or embody the words of the sages. By truly making them his own, he himself can become sage-like.

It should be clear that for Zhu Xi, the study of the canon is important not principally as an intellectual exercise but as the intellectual means to a moral—even spiritual—end. Through the classical texts, especially the Four Books, the sensitive reader can apprehend the principle underlying the universe and hence, as Zhu writes, "practice the Way with all his strength, and so enter the realm of the sages and worthies." The investigation of things thus may be directed toward things in the world "out there," especially the Four Books, but it is a process that takes as its ultimate aim internal moral cultivation. By apprehending the principle that inheres in things, we awaken fully the principle that is our human nature, and thereby give full expression in our daily lives to the true goodness, righteousness, ritual propriety, and wisdom, endowed in each and every one of us at birth. Probing principle to "its limit" is simply to perfect oneself morally.

The "Neo" in Neo-Confucianism

A religious or philosophical tradition endures because of its ability to adapt and remain relevant over time. One that is unable to respond to a changing world necessarily becomes moribund. The famous longevity of the Confucian tradition is attributable in large degree to its elasticity, to its effectiveness in shaping its message to address the pressing issues of the day. The "Learning of the Way," or Neo-Confucianism, exemplifies the capacity of the Confucian school to engage in ongoing reinterpretation of its fundamental teachings. Eleventh- and twelfth-century reflection on the Confucian tradition and the revered canonical texts yields an understanding of that Confucian message that is meaningful and relevant to an eleventh- and twelfth-century audience. This is an audience, which following the introduction of other schools in the first millennium, such as "Mysterious Learning" (*xuanxue*, 玄學, once commonly rendered as Neo-Daoism) and Buddhism, has become accustomed to thinking about the metaphysical nature of the cosmos, man's place in it, and man's capacity for understanding and accessing the true reality of the universe.

A brief list of ways that eleventh- and twelfth-century "Neo"-Confucianism is "new" or different from classical Confucianism would include:

- the use of a language of metaphysics;
- the placement of man in the context of a universe of principle and *qi*;
- the introduction of "the investigation of things," probing principle as *the* basis of the Confucian self-cultivation process;
- a narrowing of focus with an emphasis on man's interior life;

- the establishment of a set program of learning, privileging the Four Books over the Five Classics.

The metaphysical cast of the Neo-Confucian system, in particular, can make it challenging to appreciate that this later school of Confucianism indeed shares classical Confucianism's most fundamental beliefs:

- that man is morally perfectible;
- that learning is key to moral improvement;
- that the sages of antiquity provide a Way to be moral and behave appropriately in society;
- that the morally superior man has a transforming effect on others (*Daxue*, ch. 4);
- that social harmony is the result of people fulfilling the moral responsibilities of their roles.

The Neo-Confucian school may thus incorporate a metaphysical terminology of principle and *qi* into its teachings, but the school ultimately reaffirms—and promulgates for a contemporary eleventh- and twelfth-century audience—the moral-ethical teachings that lie at the heart of the early Confucianism of Confucius, Mencius, and Xunzi.

Neo-Confucianism after Zhu Xi

Over the course of the thirteenth and fourteenth centuries, Zhu Xi's Neo-Confucian synthesis would establish itself as *the* Chinese intellectual and political orthodoxy. Challenges to his teachings did, however, emerge. Most notably, in the fifteenth century, Wang Yangming (王陽明) (1472–1529) developed a competing variety of Neo-Confucian thought. Initially a follower of Zhu Xi's teachings and program of self-cultivation, Wang concluded that Zhu's approach to moral perfection was too bookish and his process of investigating things too onerous. He proposed that "principle is identical with the mind," and *not* with human nature, as Zhu had insisted.

The implications were great. No longer was there a need for students to engage in the protracted study of the canon or to seek to apprehend principle in the world "out there." In Wang's understanding, the "extension of knowledge" from the *Great Learning* did not refer to the expansion of one's knowledge of principle through *external* investigation. Instead, it referred to the extension or application of one's *inborn* moral mind—one's innate faculty for knowing Confucian right from wrong—to every thing, affair, and situation one encounters. For Wang, to learn right from wrong, to conduct oneself properly in all of life's circumstances, did not depend on undergoing an arduous program of learning; rather, it required only that one be mindful in what one does, exercising the good moral—and Confucian—conscience with which every human being is born.

One obvious appeal of the Wang Yangming school was to make moral self-realization considerably more accessible than Zhu had, since canonical literacy and study were no longer essential. The Zhu Xi school maintained, in theory, that anyone could achieve moral perfection, but in practice its program of rigorous classical learning limited the field to those who had the good fortune, means, and leisure to devote themselves to study. In sum, Wang's teachings offered—at least in theory—the possibility of Confucian self-cultivation to the unlettered, or as Wang himself put it, to "ignorant" men and women.

The Zhu Xi school would be the dominant school of Neo-Confucianism in China through the early decades of the twentieth century; its doctrines and commentaries would serve as the foundations of the educational curriculum. But Wang's school would also achieve considerable popularity, especially in the later years of the Ming dynasty (1368–1644). And as their teachings made their way to Korea and Japan, both the Zhu Xi and Wang Yangming schools of Neo-Confucianism would find loyal and enthusiastic followers beyond the borders of the Middle Kingdom.

Chapter 6
Confucianism in practice

Thus far we have seen Confucius "transmit" an idealized sociopolitical vision from the early Zhou past; we have seen faithful followers elaborate on this vision and, in the process, give it different emphases and meanings; and we have seen thinkers more than a millennium after his death reorient this vision, explaining its significance in the context of a universe of principle and *qi*, philosophical terms that would have meant little to Confucius himself. Our focus has been mainly on the realm of ideas, looking at how the original vision of the Master has been given a variety of interpretive shapes over the centuries.

These teachings, however, did not remain confined to the realm of ideas. They played out in the ritual practice of the people, in the everyday life of the family, in the moral education of peasants and elite alike, and in the administration of the state. It may be an oversimplification to characterize premodern Chinese society and politics as "Confucian"—suggesting more of an exclusivity than is warranted—but to say they were heavily "Confucianized," informed and guided by principles of the Confucian persuasion, is entirely apt.

The "Institutionalization" of Confucianism

As early as the Han dynasty, Confucianism would be made an important ideological prop of the Chinese state. As we saw in chapter 1, Emperor Wu, upon ascending the throne in 141 BCE, decreed that all non-Confucians be dismissed from office; and a few years later, in 124 BCE he founded the Imperial Academy, which took as its core curriculum the Five Classics. Students at the academy who demonstrated their familiarity with one or more of the Classics through end-of-year examinations would become expectant officials, filling positions in the bureaucracy as they became vacant.

Until this time, Confucianism had been just one among many schools of thought. But with the measures taken under Emperor Wu, it assumed a central role in China's official ideology. By the tenth century or so, with the more regular use of the civil service examinations, it would become *the* dominant teaching, a sort of state orthodoxy. Thus beginning in the second century BCE, the Chinese state was increasingly a "Confucian" one—a state administered by a Confucian elite whose policies and principles of governance were rooted, at least ideally, in Confucian teachings. (Of course, as with Western Christendom, a considerable disjuncture frequently existed between the ideals of the Chinese state and its actual practices.)

In the view of Confucians, official service was society's highest and most important calling. This view was reflected in their hierarchical ranking of occupations, which (though never formally legislated) exercised profound influence over the course of Chinese history. In this ranking, the (Confucian) scholar-official held the top spot; next came the farmer whose labors fed the people; then came the artisan who provided products and tools for daily use; and finally came the merchant. The merchant's ranking at the very bottom was indicative of the Confucian view of the merchant as parasitic, making and doing nothing of his own but trading in the wares of the more productive "classes"—the farmers and artisans. This disparagement of merchants would persist through most of imperial Chinese history, as Confucian values became increasingly dominant in society. (Note also that the military man figures nowhere in this hierarchy, foreshadowing the culture's privileging of the civil service over military service and the generally low esteem in which military men and their pursuits were held in the later imperial period.)

Merchants, the least socially esteemed, might amass great wealth and live in luxury and comfort, while peasants typically struggled to survive. Indeed, merchants' wealth could easily exceed that of even the most prominent officials. Such wealth, however, would never confer on merchants the social status and prestige associated with officials, and it was perhaps for this reason that successful merchants often insisted that their sons study for the examinations rather than continue in their profession. Officials, it was believed, had won appointment to the civil service through extraordinary talent and moral character—talent and character so great that they had come to the attention of the emperor himself. Called to serve, they stood at the side of the imperial presence, assisting and advising him on how to bring peace and harmony to the empire. They were the elite of society, "the stars in heaven," as a popular saying put it.

Chinese governments employed a variety of methods for recruiting civil officials. The most common were: (1) recommendation, whereby local authorities would forward the names of outstanding individuals to the capital for appointment to the civil service; (2) "appointment by protection," a privilege held by officials of a certain status to nominate one or more of their sons, or other family members, for civil service; and (3) state-sponsored examinations, success in which would lead to official status in the civil service, if not always to official appointment. Of these, it was the civil service examinations that would become the major—and by far most prestigious—avenue of recruitment.

The civil service examination system

Rulers of the Sui dynasty (589–618) extended the use of examinations, administering them throughout the empire. The following dynasty, the Tang (618–907), continued and expanded the Sui practice, holding them more regularly and bringing in larger numbers of officials—though by no means the majority—through the examination process. But it was the later Tang practice of awarding those successful in the examinations with the highest offices that gave the examination system decisive momentum. By the ninth century, even those who might have won a civil appointment through hereditary privilege felt it necessary to sit for the examinations if they were ever to obtain a position of real importance. Henceforth, for a full millennium, until the early years of the twentieth century, the road to elite status in China was through the examination system.

From the time of its maturity in the late Tang to the early twentieth century, the examination system was based almost entirely on what had come to be identified as Confucian teachings; its purpose, after all, was to recruit officials who could assist in governing a state that defined itself as Confucian. The particular form that examinations would take, and the particular weighting given to different features of the examination (e.g., explications of the Classics, poetic composition, policy questions, prose style, calligraphy), might change over the centuries, but the knowledge tested on the examinations remained steadfastly Confucian. Prior to the thirteenth century, candidates were expected to demonstrate mastery of the Five Classics in particular; they were the core of the examination curriculum. In 1313, with the growing influence of the Zhu Xi school, the government decreed a change, announcing that the Four Books, and in particular Zhu Xi's understanding of the Four Books, would now serve as the basis of the examinations.

It is hard to exaggerate the influence that the examination system exercised in Chinese society. Children would begin their education

A CHINESE BOY'S SCHOOL (CHRISTIAN).

5. A nineteenth-century Chinese classroom. Students standing in front of the teacher's desk are "backing the book," that is, reciting the text aloud by rote.

in the home, typically under the tutelage of their mothers, with Confucian primers like the *Three Character Classic*. If they continued with their schooling—as only a very small percentage of Chinese children did due to limited family resources—by the age of seven or so they would embark on the study of the *Great Learning*, the *Analects*, the *Mencius*, and *Maintaining Perfect Balance* under a private tutor or a village teacher. The learning process would be arduous and not necessarily intellectually challenging or stimulating. Most time would be spent in rote memorization, in the exercise of "backing the book." In "backing the book," a pupil would approach the teacher's desk, and with his back to the teacher recite aloud, from memory, the line or lines the teacher had asked him to prepare. If his recitation was flawless, he would return to his desk and begin work on the next line in the text. But if he forgot a word or confused word order, then with the *thwack* of a bamboo rod, he would be ordered back to his seat to continue his memorization efforts. This learning regimen ensured that by the time he was fifteen he would "know" the Four Books; he would be capable of reciting each of them front-to-back, line-by-line, without error.

Come age fifteen, if his talent was deemed sufficient and if his family's resources were ample enough, he would likely continue with his education, focusing his aim now on the civil service examinations. The chances of winning the highest degree in the examinations, the *jinshi* (進士) or "presented scholar" degree, were slim indeed. A candidate first had to pass the prefectural-level examinations; success there would entitle him to sit for the provincial-level examinations, held triennially; success at the provincial level, in turn, permitted him to move on to the imperial capital and compete in the metropolitan examination, held triennially as well.

Studies indicate that less than 1 percent of those sitting for the district examinations would ultimately pass the metropolitan examinations. And yet, even in the face of such long odds, virtually all literate Chinese would start down the examination path. The most ambitious among them hoped to earn the *jinshi* degree, which almost guaranteed official appointment, wealth, and high status in late imperial Chinese society. Many others, aware that their chances of "hitting the bull's eye" (that is, gaining *jinshi* status) were quite slim, embarked on examination study because of other benefits the system offered. *Shengyuan* (生員) candidates who succeeded in the first major set of examinations at the prefectural level, although not yet eligible for office, were rewarded with certain privileges: exemption from corvée labor and corporeal punishment. In addition, holders of *shengyuan* status (and even more of *juren* [舉人] status, the next step up) could claim some degree of learning and knowledge of the great texts of the Chinese tradition, assets that would aid them in a variety of professions—teaching, business, and estate management among them—and in the forging of useful social networks.

The pressure to succeed in these examinations was as great as their allure. Candidates had given years, even decades, to examination preparation. Many had failed the provincial or metropolitan examinations repeatedly, only to return again for the next round. Indeed, among those successful in winning a *jinshi* degree at the capital the average age was in the mid-thirties. The onerous years dedicated to examination life by persevering candidates became fertile material for Chinese satirists and fiction writers. And no matter how well prepared or how deep and genuine their knowledge of Confucian teachings, candidates knew all too well their meager statistical chances. Not surprisingly, many would look for a competitive edge—and that edge was not necessarily always on the up-and-up.

6. The examination compound in Canton in ca. 1873. On entering the compound the candidate would be assigned a "cell" number in one of the marked rows. This compound contains 7,500 cells.

Candidates might resort to one of any number of common cheating techniques, including (1) wearing undergarments with the text of the Classics or exemplary examinations essays inscribed on them; (2) wrapping cheat-sheets in their food and bedding; (3) hiring an "impersonator"—an experienced, more accomplished essayist—to assume their identity and take their place in their assigned cell; (4) buying the examination question in advance from an official examiner; (5) bribing an examiner; and (6) arranging for someone inside or outside the compound to compose an answer to the question once it had been announced and pass that answer to them in their cell. Measures were constantly introduced by the state to prevent against these abuses and the many others that grew up around the system. But candidates could be resourceful, and given the rewards that

7. An undergarment with hundreds of model examination essays written in tiny characters. "Cheat shirts" like this, inscribed with the text of the Confucian classics or model essays, might be sewn into the lining of a candidate's robe and "consulted" during the examinations.

were sure to come with success, the temptation to boost their chances proved too great. Corruption was a constant throughout the system's history. The irony here is profound: in an examination system whose explicit purpose it was to seek out those in the empire with the best understanding of Confucian moral-ethical teachings, cheating would become epidemic.

Still, it was this system that fostered the transmission of the moral ideals and practices associated with Confucianism throughout Chinese society. As I have suggested, most education in China was geared toward examination learning and, consequently, reinforced the values promoted in the examinations. School children, whether they lived in Beijing, Xi'an, or Guangzhou, read the same Confucian primers and the same Four Books and Five Classics; and in reading the Four Books and Five Classics, they all read the commentary declared orthodox by the state. Similarly, the literate elite, whether sitting for exams in Zhejiang province, Shandong province, or Sichuan province, had all mastered the same canonical works and, it was hoped, had all come to embody Confucian virtues and ideals in the process. It was these virtues and ideals they were expected to uphold if they were fortunate enough to win official appointment. This is to say that the examination system served as a powerfully integrative force in Chinese history. It ensured that as far-flung as Chinese territory was, as large and diverse as the population might have been, there nonetheless would exist a widely shared culture, a system of values, beliefs, and customs that would create a semblance of unity among the people and make them more readily governable from an imperial center.

Interestingly, although the examinations promoted the values and interests of the Confucian school, beginning in the Tang dynasty the examination system was subject to a litany of critiques by Confucian literati themselves. Common objections to the system included:

- It rewarded rote memorization and adherence to rigid literary regulation, not originality or analytical thinking.

- It promoted bookish, antiquarian knowledge, not knowledge of practical use in governing the country.

- It was not an effective means of assessing the moral character of candidates; a system of recommendations would be more effective in finding men of good character and thus should replace or supplement the examination system.

- It distracted students from genuine learning, which is to say learning for the sake of moral cultivation; instead, learning had come to serve the pursuit of hollow fame and worldly success.

- It induced heated and vulgar competition, and a good Confucian is not supposed to compete, according to Confucius.

These objections were not dismissed out of hand and at times provoked serious debate. Indeed, over the centuries the examination system underwent frequent change and reform. Still, as a system it persevered intact for nearly fifteen hundred years and was a most powerful force in shaping and sustaining China's cultural and social norms. It was the very foundation of Chinese imperial order.

Confucianism and the common people

If the scholar-official elite could be called Confucian, what about the common people, those who had no access to education? How "Confucian" were they? They clearly shared many of the beliefs and ideals associated with Confucius and his tradition. Most, no doubt, recognized (even if they did not necessarily fulfill) their filial obligations to parents and grandparents; and most who could afford to celebrate their ancestral line through ritual offerings probably did so. Chinese society encouraged elite and non-elite, by means both formal and informal, to adopt the social practices and beliefs sanctioned by the state: Village schools instructed children, even those who would not go on to serious examination study, in basic Confucian teachings and principles;

local officials and village elders read aloud from proclamations and so-called community compacts that promoted proper social behavior; emperors circulated moral instructions, Confucian in tone and sentiment, throughout the empire; and families observed the family and ancestral rites codified by the Confucian school and passed on from generation to generation.

Whether the common people, socialized in the values and practices of the dominant culture, would have identified these values and practices as "Confucian" is doubtful. More likely they would have simply regarded them as the favored conventions of Chinese culture. Yet in being filial toward parents, respectful toward elders, and reverential toward ancestors, they were embracing practices and ideals that by the second century BCE had come to be closely associated with Confucian teachings. In characterizing China's non-elite, I propose that we err on the side of caution: most could not be called "Confucian" in that they did not give themselves to the study of Confucian teachings or identify in any substantive manner as followers of the Confucian school; and yet the lives they lived were in no small measure shaped by the teachings and practices of Confucianism.

Indeed, distinguishing between "Confucian" and "Chinese" can be historically challenging for students of China. Take filial piety. It was a centerpiece of the teachings of Confucius. No person in imperial China could reasonably claim to be a "Confucian" follower and at the same time expressly turn his back on the value of filial piety. Yet this value was in place long before Confucius celebrated it. When Confucius remarks to his disciples, "I transmit and create nothing of my own" (7.1), filial piety would have been just one of many of the tradition's teachings and practices he had in mind. So, is filial piety "Chinese" because its origins are deep within the Chinese cultural past and pre-date the emergence of Confucius and his school? Or is it "Confucian" because Confucius, in selecting from the past, gives new relevance and life to an ideal at risk and ensures its ongoing diffusion among the Chinese people through its integral association with the Confucian orthodoxy of the state? I would argue that it is both.

In any event, when I refer in this book to those ideals appropriated by Confucius from the earlier Chinese tradition as "Confucian," I trust the reader will recognize that I am not suggesting either that their origins lie with the Master or that their practice is limited to his true followers. The orthodox status attained by his teachings guaranteed them a wide, general diffusion in Chinese society.

Confucianism and the ruler

The tradition of one-man rule in China dates back to long before the institutionalization of Confucianism in the second century BCE, to no later than 1400 BCE, when inscriptions on oracle bones attest to the authority and power of Shang kings. But Confucian teachings' high praise for the virtues of one-man rule no doubt lent further legitimacy to China's traditional system of monocratic governance.

Confucius, of course, assumed that one-man rule would be effective because the ruler acted as *paterfamilias*, a benign and gentle authority guiding his subjects as a father would his children, with affection and concern for their well-being. His monocratic rule was justified by his perfect virtue and the moral charisma that naturally attracted the loyalty and obedience of his subject "children"—the common people who did not have the education or virtue to govern themselves. Through his goodness and exemplary ritual practice he would teach them proper behavior and a respect for hierarchical order, and thereby establish harmony throughout the realm. And just as a father was expected to make decisions on behalf of his family, so too was the ruler expected to make decisions on behalf of his people. The ideal government for Confucius was government *for* the people, but not *of* or *by* the people.

If the ruler were indeed benevolent, this system would work quite well. But, in fact, the sort of ruler idealized by Confucius would hardly have been typical. The question arises: How, according to the Confucian system, would the political order operate effectively in the absence of a truly good Confucian ruler? Confucius, to be sure, believed and hoped that Confucian-trained officials would be a check on the ruler's power—and provide the direction he needed. But the fact remained that the bureaucracy was staffed with "his" men. They had come to office through his beneficence, through success in the examinations that his government sponsored and an additional palace examination that he personally had overseen. The emperor was responsible for appointing and dismissing them; even exiling or killing them was entirely his prerogative. This is not to say that scholar-officials did not offer criticism of imperial decisions, but they did so at great personal risk. Challenges to the authority of the emperor were not made casually—or routinely, I imagine.

The fundamental problem in imperial Chinese history was this: when Confucian ideology proved ineffective in guiding and constraining the imperial will, there was little recourse. There were no constitutional or legal limits on the power or conduct of the emperor and no institutions or offices with legitimate authority to check imperial behavior when it veered far from Confucian ideals. As a consequence, rulers could—and at times did—abuse their power or neglect their responsibilities with impunity.

Take the case of the first emperor of the Ming, Taizu (r. 1368–98), a commoner who came to the throne as the leader of a rebel movement. Barely literate, he is said to have had a deep distrust—and envy—of the highly educated scholar-official class. In 1380, suspicious that his prime minister was plotting to overthrow him, Taizu abolished the secretariat—the central administrative organ of government—and took over personal and direct control of virtually all aspects of government. The opinion of Confucian scholar-officials carried no weight. Those officials who displeased him he had flogged and beaten with clubs (often to death) in full view of the court. Under Taizu, benevolent, paternalistic rule gave way to cruel, sometimes savage despotism.

The Tianqi emperor (r. 1620–27) was a ruler of the negligent variety, preferring to spend his days at carpentry, making fine furniture, rather than oversee the administration of the realm. His disregard—indeed distaste—for affairs of state gave the court eunuch Wei Zongxian the opportunity to seize control of government. Wei proceeded quickly to fill positions of power with opportunistic cronies, levy exploitative taxes on the people, and conduct a brutal purge of hundreds of scholar-officials who dared oppose him. In short, Tianqi's imperial disinterest resulted in a notorious regime of terror, from which the dynasty never recovered. Within two decades of Wei's rise to power, the Ming collapsed.

These cases are somewhat extreme but are offered to make the point that (because there existed no constitutional checks) bad things could happen when those at the highest levels of government did not embrace Confucian ideals. Most of the time, however, even if rulers and officials did not fully embody Confucian ideals, they were sufficiently able and competent to oversee the affairs of the state and defend the interests of their dynasty.

Confucianism and the family

As we saw in chapter 2, Confucius makes a case in the *Analects* for the foundational importance of the family in Chinese society, arguing that it is the locus of moral-ethical assimilation. It is here that the individual learns to be "Chinese," that he is introduced to the values, customs, and practices that distinguish Chinese people from the rest of the "barbarian" world. And it is here that he is introduced to the normative hierarchy of society: that senior generations are superior to junior ones; that older people are superior to younger ones; and that males are superior to females.

The family was patrilineal, meaning simply that the family line was traced through the male from a founding male ancestor. Children, although descended from both a mother and father, inherited their family membership from the father. The family's descent line thus would continue only if the family continued to produce male offspring. It is for this reason that the birth of a son was from the earliest times in Chinese history regarded as a "great happiness," while the birth of a daughter was considered but a "small happiness." A son could carry on the family line; a daughter would marry "out" into her husband's family, with the principal responsibility of ensuring the continuity of his family line for another generation. In a remark that would echo through the ages, Mencius said, "There are three ways to be unfilial, and the worst is to have no heir" (*Mencius* 4A.26).

What were the consequences of a family line coming to an end? Most grievous was that there would be no one to care for the ancestors. And the importance of ancestors in Chinese culture can hardly be overstated. These ancestors were entirely responsible for a person's existence. Without his father, and his father's father, and the generations of fathers before his father's father, a man simply would not be. His feeling of indebtedness to generations past was to be repaid with reverential treatment of their spirits through the performance of the so-called ancestral rites. These rites, passed down through texts like the canonical *Book of Rites* and the *Family Rituals* (compiled by the Neo-Confucian thinker Zhu Xi), kept alive the memory of the ancestors and sustained them in their existence in the spirit realm. When the rites came to an end, so too did the memory and spirits of the ancestors.

Of course, in the Judeo-Christian-Islamic West, forebears commanded devotion, affection, and respect as well. But there is a fundamental difference between these Western Abrahamic traditions and the Chinese Confucian tradition. In the West, the one God was thought responsible for the creation of all that was and all that is. It was God who created humankind in the form of

Adam and Eve; it was thus God who was ultimately responsible for the existence of all human beings. To be sure, people bound to these traditions honored their family line, but their highest show of reverence and respect went to God, who first created their family line. In a culture where an indigenous belief in a creator deity did not exist—and where a foreign belief in one did not become widespread—it was the biological line alone that accounted for one's existence and deserved the gratitude and praise of the individual.

Like all other normative relationships in China, that between ancestor and descendant is built on the principle of reciprocity. Just as parents and grandparents guide and protect the young, ancestors, too, continue to provide guidance and protection for the family. They do what they can to ensure good fortune, good

8. Family members paying respects to their ancestors at the family altar. (The family here appears to be posing for the photographer, as normally they would be facing the altar)

harvests, and good child-bearing, and in return, on their birthdays and other commemorative occasions, the family pays respects to the ancestral spirits, placing offerings of foodstuffs (e.g., oranges, pork, liquor, and sweets) and provisions (e.g., playing cards, scrolls, tobacco, a paper model of a fine carriage) that the ancestors were known to have enjoyed in life on the family altar in the home. If it is a family from a well-to-do lineage (in Chinese terms, a lineage is made up of all the family branches that trace their descent from a single male ancestor), the offerings are placed in the offering hall at the lineage temple. Failure to remember an ancestor, it was thought, could to lead to misfortune—family illness, diseased crops, or a failed business venture. Attending to the neglected ancestor, remembering him dutifully in accord with the rites, might bring some relief or improvement to the troubles the family was experiencing.

This raises another striking difference with mainstream Western tradition. In the West, the gulf between this world and the "other world" is vast. An unfamiliar, immaterial God resides over the "other world." God is omnipotent, not bound by obligations of reciprocity. And God is ultimately unknowable, meaning too that God's plans for humankind are not fully unknowable. Hence in praying to God and looking beyond this world for guidance and hope, people are told that they must have faith. In the Chinese tradition, it is Second Uncle Feng and Grandpa Feng who reside in the other world. There is little about Second Uncle and Grandpa that is unfamiliar—or immaterial—to the younger generations of Fengs. The younger Fengs received instruction and counsel from them beginning in childhood. They shared meals with them and knew their favorite dishes. They joined them in all of the important family occasions—cappings, weddings, funerals, and ancestral ceremonies. And they helped care for them in their old age. The younger Fengs, in turning to the world beyond theirs, could be confident that the spirits of Second Uncle and Grandpa remained invested in the well-being of the family and would do all they could to benefit its members and protect them from harm.

This is to say that in China the "other-world" was not very "otherly" or remote. It is perhaps best, then, to understand the Chinese spirit world not as an "other" world but rather as part of a continuum in the world of the family.

The ancestral rites, whether performed at a modest altar in the family home or in a large offering hall in a lineage temple, serve multiple functions. They give expression to the family's indebtedness for all that previous generations provided, including, most importantly, life itself; they preserve the memory of the ancestors and sustain their vitality in the spirit world; they lessen the fear of death, demonstrating to the living that when *they* part from this world they will continue to play a role in the life of the family; and they cement family bonds—and enhance the family's corporate identity—by bringing the members together to commemorate their shared ancestry.

The focus here on sacrifice and the expression of reverence to ancestors is not meant to suggest that Chinese did not believe in gods and spirits. There were gods and spirits of the natural world, presiding over rivers, mountains, winds, seasons, and the like. And there were gods and spirits who provided assistance and comfort to practitioners of Daoism, Buddhism, and popular religious sects. But the belief in ancestral spirits—and the ceremonial respect shown them—was dominant in Chinese society, widely shared by almost all people (including those who considered themselves Daoists and Buddhists), irrespective of social or economic status.

Confucianism and women

Confucius said, "Women and petty men (*xiaoren*) are especially hard to handle" (17.23). Although many interpreters over the centuries have tried to soften the thrust of this remark, there is no getting away from its general disparagement of women. Indeed, nowhere in the *Analects* or other canonical texts is there the suggestion that the Confucian program for self-cultivation and moral perfection was applicable to women. The teachings of Confucius—and those of most of his later followers—were seemingly intended for men.

The assumption that they did not have comparable moral potential as men meant that in the Confucian view, women had no place in public life—a prejudice that would persist until the twentieth century. Never were women permitted to serve as civil officials, nor were they ever allowed to enter the examination compound. Their responsibilities were to be limited to the "inner quarters," to matters within the household.

This is not to say that women did not wield political power. But the power they exercised derived not from their own legitimate, institutionalized authority but from their proximity to a powerful male. Chinese history is filled with women who as consorts, wives, and mothers to magistrates, ministers, and emperors possessed considerable political influence. One need only think here of Empress Dowager Cixi (1835-1908) who controlled the Qing court for the entire second half of the nineteenth century, first as mother to the Tongzhi emperor (r. 1862-74), then as aunt to the Guangxu emperor (1875-1908, whom she herself appointed), and finally, after 1898, as de facto ruler. In fact, there was one truly notable exception to the rule—Empress Wu [r. 690-705] of the Tang dynasty. In 690, having been Emperor Gaozong's [r. 649-83] empress, Empress Wu ascended the throne and proclaimed herself the "Son of Heaven." She would be the first—and the last—female Son of Heaven in China's long history.

Though they might never sit for an exam or become a scholar-official, girls growing up in an elite household would commonly learn to read the Confucian primers and texts such as the *Analects*, the *Mencius*, the *Book of Poetry*, the *Book of Filial Piety,* and *Lessons for Women* by Ban Zhao of the Han dynasty. It was supposed that exposure to these works and their teachings would help make them into model, virtuous Confucian women. It was supposed, too, that literacy among girls in the family would enhance the family's status, indicating that it had the resources and cultural investment in educating its daughters as well as its sons. But there was an additional motivating force for providing instruction to girls: it made them more marriageable, which is to say more attractive to families looking for brides, who, as mothers, could take on the role of teaching their young sons the basic Confucian texts. Few girls in non-elite families would receive an education; rather, they would learn to carry out the domestic chores that would be theirs to do for much of the rest of their lives: sewing, weaving, cooking, cleaning, and perhaps farming the fields.

For a girl, marriage was *the* life-changing event. On her wedding day, the bride, typically in her mid-to-late teens, would leave her family's household for the groom's household to live there with his parents, his still unmarried sisters, his brothers, their wives, and their children. Arriving at the gate of groom's house or estate, she would bow to the senior generations of the groom's family and to the memory of the family's ancestors. Henceforth, his family would be hers; and his ancestors would be hers. It was to them, not to her birth family's ancestors, that she would sacrifice and pay reverence. She herself now belonged to the groom's family line.

The loss of identity that came with this transition to the husband's family must have been traumatic for many. Consider: the wedding day may have been the first time a bride set eyes not simply on her husband's extended family but on her husband himself. She had not known him and had played no part in arranging the union with him. The union was an agreement reached by his parents and her parents, perhaps with the assistance of a matchmaker, based on what served the mutual interests of the two families. It was decidedly *not* a contract of love entered into freely by wife and husband.

So here we have a very junior female entering into an unfamiliar household, with a jumble of new relationships to negotiate. There were the parents-in-law, the brothers-in-law, the sisters-in-law, the nieces, and the nephews, not to mention the possible servants, maids, concubines, cooks, and the like. Living now under one roof with them, it was essential that she get along with them—if only because it would make her new life easier.

From her natal family and from the teachings of Ban Zhao in *Lessons for Women,* the young bride had learned what was most necessary to "succeed" in her new family: to serve her parents-in-law dutifully, to obey their every command. The mother-in-law and the father-in-law were now her parents. Her principal responsibility was to please them, especially the mother-in-law, by every means possible. In *Lessons for Women* she had read:

> Nothing is better than an obedience that sacrifices personal opinion. Whenever the mother-in-law says, "Do not do that," and if what she says is right, unquestionably the daughter-in-law obeys. Whenever the mother-in-law says, "Do that," even if what she says is wrong, still the daughter-in-law submits unfailingly to the command. Let a woman not act contrary to the wishes and opinions of parents-in-law about right and wrong; let her not dispute with them what is straight and what is crooked. Such (docility) may be called obedience that sacrifices personal opinion.

It was important that as the outsider entering into the family, the daughter-in-law subordinate her will to the family's. Only by doing so might she, with time, gain welcome acceptance into it.

Some in-law families might be kinder, gentler, and more welcoming to the new bride and some less so. But they all had precisely the same expectation of this outsider: that she bear the husband's children and continue the family line—now her family line. Of course, she had been raised by her birth parents to understand as well that this was her obligation when she married.

So on entering her new household she knew what the expectations of her were; and she knew that the sooner she met them, the sooner her lot as an outsider in the family would likely improve. And because nothing would improve it more than producing an heir, she hoped, just as the in-laws did, that the child would be a boy. Their "big happiness" would be her "big happiness."

Having children did not simply improve her lot in her new family. When she had "married out," she had left behind all the emotional richness of her natal family; entering into the husband's family, she was little more than a stranger on probation in a sense. Likely, her existence there had been largely devoid of emotional fulfillment and bonds of real affection. Now, with a child or children of her own, her life would be much enriched emotionally—and much less lonely. Within the larger patrilineal family of her in-laws she had created her own close-knit "uterine family"—as some anthropologists call it—in which she at last could expect to enjoy some degree of emotional intimacy. (She might also imagine a day when she would become a mother-in-law to her sons' wives and enjoy the authority, respect, and privileged treatment her own mother-in-law enjoyed.)

It was her place as mother to provide instruction for the young children. She was to be their first teacher. The *Analects for Women*, a ninth-century text outlining the "Confucian Way for women" (*fudao,* 婦道), asserts: "Most all families have sons and daughters.... The responsibility to instruct them rests solely with the mother." The mother's instruction was to take the form of modeling good behavior and recounting stories, historical events, and anecdotes from the tradition that taught Confucian morality. Additionally, mothers who were literate would recite aloud the *Lessons for Women*, the *Analects*, the *Mencius*, the *Book of Filial Piety*, and other staple works to their children. Such recitation served a dual purpose: it furthered the moral development of the children and introduced to them the canonical texts their families hoped they (especially the boys) would someday master.

9. **A lithographic illustration from *Wu Youru huabao* (1908, rpt. 1983) of a mother teaching her son to write**

In the domestic sphere, then, the woman played the roles of dutiful daughter-in law and moral instructress. But she played yet another role, important and yet only infrequently mentioned in the scholarly literature—that of household manager. The *Analects for Women* states:

> A woman who manages the household should be thrifty and diligent. If she is diligent, the household thrives; if lazy, it declines. If she is thrifty, the household become enriched; if extravagant, it becomes impoverished.

In an elite household, the responsibilities associated with managing the household could be especially daunting and might include tracking the family finances; maintaining order among the various sons and their wives; apportioning their monthly allowances; supervising the domestic help and paying each his or her monthly "stipend"; overseeing the kitchen, which meant seeing to the purchase of all food provisions and the feeding of all members of the household; and, if it was a landowning family, collecting rents from tenants. In such a household the husband, disdainful of dirtying his hands over money matters and mundane domestic chores, most likely retreated to his study, leaving all these tasks to his wife. He might also well be away from home serving as an official, conducting business, or simply enjoying a spell in the city.

A woman's marriage was expected to be a lifelong commitment, continuing beyond the death of her husband—whether death struck at old age or in his teens. Confucian teachings viewed remarriage as a disgrace, likening a twice-married woman to a disloyal minister who serves two lords. When she married, she had not simply entered into a relationship with the groom but into a relationship with his entire family. His death thus did not bring an end to her responsibilities to the family. Were her parents-in-law still alive, her duty to serve them persisted; and were her children, or her children's children, living in the household, her duty to nurture and instruct them persisted. The Confucian tradition—and associated texts like the *Analects for Women*—required the faithful wife to remain chaste until the end of her days. The state embraced and promoted this ideal, building stone commemorative arches (some of which still stand) to honor those widowed women whose deeds had won them particular renown for chastity.

If we were to read only the normative writings for women—works like Ban Zhao's *Lessons for Women* and the *Analects for Women*—it would be easy to assume that women were passive, submissive creatures, ruthlessly subordinated first to the demands of their fathers and mothers and then to the demands of their husbands and in-laws. Yet within the family they could be a commanding force. A passage from a nineteenth-century instruction manual for women by Zeng Jifen (1852–1942), a daughter of the illustrious Confucian statesman Zeng Guofan (1811–72), speaks eloquently, even if perhaps self-interestedly, to the central role played by the wife in the fate of the Chinese Confucian family:

> To whom, then, does the responsibility of ruling the family members belong? I say the wife.... The wife is the one who rules inside of the house. There is not even one matter of the entire family that is not closely related to the wife. These matters cannot be delegated to the husband. Why can't the husband rule the home? I say, he does not have the free time. Also, his ambitions lie everywhere but with the home. Regardless of whether he is a scholar or peasant, artisan or merchant, the husband wishes to devote all of his talents to making a living outside of the house. He exhausts his intelligence, accumulates wealth, relies on the wife for management, and keeps to it in order to establish the family. Thus the rise and fall of a family's destiny is completely tied to whether the wife is worthy or not.

Although polemical, to be sure, this remark cautions us against concluding that because the recorded regulations governing women's behavior in Chinese society emphasized their subordination, women were without power or authority in pre-modern China. Some women were able—much to the distress of Confucian commentators—to exert influence, and even to dominate, in the political realm. Still more to the point, within the family, the basic unit of Chinese society, women were granted legitimate access to authority, as mothers, teachers, and household managers.

Epilogue:
Confucianism in the twentieth and twenty-first centuries

The pervasive influence that Confucian teachings had on pre-modern Chinese politics, society, and thought would meet with harsh condemnation in the early decades of the twentieth century by leaders of the nationalist May Fourth movement. Distressed by a century of assaults on Chinese sovereignty by Western imperialist powers and Japan—and by the ineffectuality of China's recently established republican government (1912–49)—students and workers in China staged mass protests beginning on May 4, 1919. These May Fourth reformers dedicated themselves to building a strong and, above all else, "modern" China capable of taking its place in the world. To build this modern China, they first sought the source of their nation's weakness. They found that source in Confucianism.

In the late 1910s and the 1920s, they launched a frontal attack on the Confucian tradition, insisting that "Mr. Confucius" and his antiquated customs and beliefs had to go if China truly wished to become a strong and healthy society. "Down with Confucius" and "smash the Old Curiosity Shop of Confucius," they chanted. An entirely new order was needed; and while liberals like Hu Shi (1891–1962) and Marxists like Chen Duxiu (1879–1942) could disagree over the particular form this new world order should take, they were of one mind that it was time to abandon Mr. Confucius in favor of Mr. Democracy and Mr. Science.

In 1918 Lu Xun (1881–1936), perhaps the greatest Chinese writer of the twentieth century, published the short story "Diary of a Madman" as a call to his fellow countrymen to throw off the shackles of Confucian culture. He tells of a madman who spent a whole night reading history, and in this history the words "true goodness, righteousness, and morality" appeared on every page. But as the night wore on, and his reading continued, the madman "began to see the words between the lines, the whole book being filled with the two words—'Eat People.'" "Diary of a Madman" was a savage condemnation of the Confucian tradition. Dressing itself up in the pieties of goodness and righteousness, Confucianism, in actuality, cannibalized and destroyed people; its hierarchical structure, which insisted that children be filial, that women be subordinate, and that inferiors be obedient to superiors, robbed people of their autonomy and vitality, and crushed the human spirit.

Events of the nineteenth century did much to shape the attitudes of intellectuals like Chen Duxiu and Lu Xun. Battered by imperialist powers beginning in 1839, China had been forced over the course of the century to open up so-called treaty ports to foreigners; to recognize the rights of these foreigners in China to be tried under their own laws (known as extraterritoriality); to pay huge indemnities to a host of imperialist powers; and to cede territory to the British and the Japanese. Chinese had come to feel strongly that their sovereign rights as a people and a nation had been grossly violated by foreign aggressors.

Statesmen and intellectuals of the late nineteenth and early twentieth centuries could agree in principle that reform was necessary if China were to meet the challenge of the Western powers and Japan. But finding a coherent program of reform they could all sign onto proved rather more difficult. Much of the disagreement occurred over the particular balance that should be struck between the adoption of Western techniques and learning and the preservation of traditional Confucian values. Undermined by such conflicts, court infighting, and heightened imperialist pressures, the efforts at reform failed. And in 1912, to a considerable extent as a result of the failure of these efforts, the Qing dynasty fell, bringing to an end a two-thousand-year history of imperial rule in China.

Leaders of the May Fourth movement showed no ambivalence about the course the country now needed to take. To establish a new strong order, China had to make a complete break with its Confucian heritage. For some in the movement, abandoning Confucianism meant looking elsewhere for intellectual traditions and political ideologies that would serve China in the twentieth century. Chen Duxiu and Li Dazhao (1888–1927), the May Fourth leaders, turned to the Russian Revolution of 1917 and the writings of Marx. As faculty at Beijing University, they organized informal Marxist study groups on campus, out of which developed a core of intellectuals increasingly knowledgeable about and dedicated to Marxist teachings. In 1921 Chen and Li would found the Chinese Communist Party (CCP) in Shanghai. The May Fourth exhortation to break with the native cultural tradition thus laid the necessary groundwork for the establishment of the Communist Party in China.

Of course, not all Chinese were eager to reject Confucianism so decisively. Some intellectuals continued to find meaning in the Confucian tradition. For instance, Liang Shuming (1893–1988), in *The Cultures of East and West and Their Philosophies* (1921), countered the May Fourthers, insisting that Chinese traditional culture, and Confucianism in particular, could—indeed must—assist in the rebuilding of China in the twentieth century. And in the hinterland areas distant from the urban centers of reform and revolution, many people still embraced and practiced Confucian values and rituals; many children there continued to read the Four Books as well as the "modern" textbooks of the new school curriculum.

The Nationalist Party, under the leadership of Chiang Kai-shek (Jiang Jieshi, 蔣介石, 1888–1975), also continued to find value in

Confucianism, especially as an ideology that could be used to combat Communism and the CCP. In 1934 Chiang launched the New Life movement, calling for the moral regeneration of the country and its people. Echoing one of Confucius's fundamental premises, he insisted that only a morally strong people could make for a strong nation—militarily, economically, and ethically. The New Life movement promoted in particular four virtues closely associated with the Confucian tradition: ritual propriety, righteousness, integrity, and a sense of shame. In his 1934 speech inaugurating the movement, Chiang said:

> The four virtues are the essential principle for the promotion of morality. They form the major rules for dealing with men and human affairs, for cultivating oneself, and for adjustment to one's surroundings. Whoever violates these rules is bound to fail, and a nation that neglects them will not survive.

The New Life movement had a short life, however, as it failed to engage the interest or support of the primarily urban populations at which it was directed. Within a couple of years it was largely forgotten, except as an indicator of the failure of the Nationalist government to unite the Chinese people behind a common ideology and national goal.

A two-decade civil war between the Nationalists led by Chiang Kai-shek and the CCP under the leadership of Mao Zedong (毛澤東) (1893–1976) came to an end in 1949, with Chiang forced to flee with his government to Taiwan. On October 1, Mao, the victor, stood atop the Gate of Heavenly Peace (Tiananmen) and proclaimed the establishment of the People's Republic of China (PRC). Mao maintained that if the proletariat was eventually to assume power in a Communist China, ongoing class struggle was essential; a harmonious society, rooted in the hierarchical relationships advocated by Confucians, was the enemy of the proletariat and the Communist state.

10. At the outset of the Cultural Revolution in 1966, Mao Zedong charged the Red Guards with destroying all vestiges of Confucianism. Here the Red Guards smash statues at the Confucius Temple in Qufu (Shandong province)

But Confucius was spared attack for the first fifteen years of PRC rule. That would change in August 1966 when Mao launched the Cultural Revolution, designed to root out those in the party who did not share his vision of how China might be transformed into a proletariat society. Urban youth, organized into groups known as the Red Guards, were called upon to make constant revolution—to destroy the bourgeois elements of society and aid Mao in purging the party leadership of his enemies. Just weeks after the Cultural Revolution was launched, Mao charged the Red Guards with demolishing the "Four Olds": old customs, old culture, old habits, and old ideas. They were left to their own to decide how to implement the Chairman's directive.

It is clear that many equated the Four Olds with Confucianism. As early as November 1966, the Red Guard Corps of Beijing Normal University had set their sights on the Confucian ancestral home in Qufu County in Shandong Province. Invoking the language of the May Fourth movement, they proceeded to Qufu, where they established themselves as the Revolutionary Rebel Liaison State to Annihilate the Old Curiosity Shop of Confucius. Within the month they had totally destroyed the Temple of Confucius, the Kong Family Mansion, the Cemetery of Confucius (including the Master's grave), and all the statues, steles, and relics in the area. On November 29 they sent a celebratory telegram to Beijing:

> Dearest Chairman Mao,
> One hundred thousand members of the revolutionary masses would like to report a thrilling development to you: We have rebelled! We have rebelled! We have dragged out the clay statue of Kong the second son (i.e., Confucius); we have torn down the plaque extolling the "teacher of ten-thousand generations"; we have leveled Confucius's grave; we have smashed the stelae extolling the virtues of feudal emperors and kings; and we have obliterated the statues in the Confucius Temple!

In January 1967 another Red Guard unit editorialized in the *People's Daily*:

> To struggle against Confucius, the feudal mummy, and thoroughly eradicate…reactionary Confucianism is one of our important tasks in the Great Cultural Revolution.

And then, to make their point, they went on a nationwide rampage, destroying temples, statues, historical landmarks, texts, and anything at all to do with the ancient Sage.

The Cultural Revolution came to an end with Mao's death in 1976. In 1978 Deng Xiaoping (1904–97) became China's paramount leader, setting China on a course of economic and political reform, and effectively bringing an end to the Maoist ideal of class conflict and perpetual revolution. Since 2000, the leadership in Beijing, eager to advance economic prosperity and promote social stability, has talked not of the need for class conflict but of the goal of achieving a "harmonious society," citing approvingly the passage from the *Analects*, "harmony is something to be cherished" (1.12). The Confucius compound in Qufu has been renovated and is now the site of annual celebrations of Confucius's birthday in late September. In recent years, colleges and universities throughout the country—Beijing University, Qufu Normal University, Renmin University, Shaanxi Normal University, and Shandong University, to name a few—have established Confucian study and research centers. And, in the opening ceremonies of the 2008 Olympics, the Beijing Olympic Committee welcomed guests from around the world to Beijing with salutations from the *Analects*, "Is it not a joy to have friends come from afar?" and "Within the fours seas all men are brothers," not with sayings from Mao's *Little Red Book*. Tellingly, when the Chinese government began funding centers to support the study of the Chinese language and culture in foreign schools and universities around the globe in 2004—a move interpreted as an effort to expand China's "soft power"—it chose to name these centers Confucius Institutes.

Many observers interpret this "endorsement" of Confucianism by the Chinese government to be part of a larger effort, in the face of mounting protests against a range of economic and social ills, to foster stability, order, and harmony. But it is not only the CCP and the government that appear to have become more favorable toward Confucius and his teachings in recent years. So too have the Chinese people. In the 1930s the Nationalists' efforts to revive Confucian values in the New Life movement met with public indifference (and in some cases, derision). Now, in the first decades of the twenty-first century, there seems to be genuine interest among the Chinese people, particularly middle-class urbanites, in embracing the teachings of the ancient sage. In 2006 a little-known professor of media studies from Beijing Normal University, Yu Dan, was invited to give a series of seven lectures on Confucianism for public television's program, "Lecture Room." Explaining the significance of the *Analects* to daily life today—in a manner accessible to non-academics—she became an overnight sensation. Her lectures struck a chord with the Chinese. When her book based on the lectures, *Yu Dan's Appreciation of the Analects*, appeared in December of that year, it sold more than 10,000 copies on the day of its release; 1.5 million copies within forty days; and more than 4 million legal copies and an estimated 6 million pirated copies by September 2007.

The success of Yu Dan's book is but one expression of the renewed interest in the native Confucian tradition. Private Confucian schools, where children from age three to twelve spend the weekend learning and memorizing the Four Books, have been cropping up around the country, as have tradition-inspired academies (*shuyuan*) and study societies (*xuetang*), where college-age students and adults come together to discuss the classical texts and their significance. Some, like the Beijing-based Yidan xuetang, ask members to go into their communities and promote a deeper appreciation of traditional Confucian values among the people—through lectures in secondary schools and colleges, group recitations of Confucian texts in public parks, and the like. Indeed, popular interest in the Confucian tradition is now such that Beijing University and Qinghua University, two of the most prestigious schools in China, offer intensive "National Study Classes" primarily for businessmen (at a cost of approximately $8,000 for thirty-six contact hours) that introduce people engaged in commerce to the Classics, most especially the Four Books.

Observers explain this twenty-first-century "revival" of popular interest in the Confucian tradition as the result of a confluence of factors. The failure of Marxism-Leninism has created an ideological vacuum, prompting people to seek new ways of understanding society and new sources of spiritual inspiration. The endemic culture of greed and corruption—spawned by the economic reforms and the celebration of wealth accompanying them—has given rise to a search for a set of values that will address these social ills. And, crucially, rising nationalist sentiments have fueled a desire to find meaning *within the native tradition*—and to offset the malignant effects of Western decadence and materialism.

Confucius has thus played a variety of roles in China's twentieth and twenty-first centuries. At times praised, at times vilified, he has been both good guy and bad guy. Yet whether good or bad, he has always been somewhere on the stage. These days Confucius appears to be gaining favor again, in official circles and among the people. But what the future holds for him and his teachings is difficult to predict. All we can say with any certainty is that Confucius will continue to matter.

References

Chapter 1: Confucius (551–479 BCE) and his legacy: An introduction

References to the *Analects* are to standard book and passage number (9.13 refers to Book 9, passage 13), as found in *A Concordance to the Analects of Confucius*, in the Harvard-Yenching Institute Sinological Index Series. Translations of the *Analects* throughout this volume are drawn from Daniel K. Gardner, *The Four Books* (Indianapolis: Hackett Publishing, 2007); D. C. Lau, *The Analects* (London: Penguin Books, 1979); James Legge, *Confucian Analects*, vol. 1, *The Chinese Classics*, rev. ed. (Hong Kong: Hong Kong University Press, 1960); Edward Slingerland, *Confucian Analects: With Selections from Traditional Commentaries* (Indianapolis: Hackett Publishing, 2003); Arthur Waley, *The Analects of Confucius* (New York: Vintage, 1989); and E. Bruce Brooks and Takeo Brooks, *The Original Analects* (New York: Columbia University Press, 1998), or are my own. For a discussion of the formation of the text of the *Analects*, see John Makeham, "On the Formation of *Lun yu* as a Book," *Monumenta Serica* 44 (1996): 1–25. The passage from Sima Qian, "Whenever a visitor wearing a Confucian hat comes" is from Burton Watson's translation, *Records of the Grand Historian of China*, 2 vols. (New York: Columbia University Press, 1961), 1:270. The exchange between Liu Bang and Lu Jia is found in Watson, *Records of the Grand Historian of China*, 1:278. On the "cosmological gulf," see Frederick Mote, *Intellectual Foundations of China*, 2nd. ed. (New York: Alfred A. Knopf, 1989), 12–25.

Chapter 2: The individual and self-cultivation in the teachings of Confucius

When speaking of self-cultivation, Confucius had in mind the self-cultivation of men, not of women. There was no expectation that women should, or could, morally perfect themselves. See chap. 6 for a discussion of women and the Confucian tradition. "There is a common saying among the people" passage is from *Mencius* 4A.5 (Book 1, Part A, passage 5), translated in Daniel K. Gardner, *The Four Books: The Basic Teachings of the Later Confucian Tradition* (Indianapolis: Hackett Publishing, 2007), 75. "From the Son of Heaven on down" passage from the *Great Learning* is translated in Gardner, *The Four Books*, 6. For a discussion of the "empirical data" Confucius finds in the early texts, see Benjamin Schwartz, *The World of Thought in Ancient China* (Cambridge, MA: Harvard University Press, 1985), 86ff. The "Now, ritual furnishes the means" passage is based on the translation in Legge, *Li Chi*, 1:63. "The parrot can speak" passage is based on the translation in Legge, *Li Chi*, 1:64–5. "Ruler and subject" passage is based on translation in Legge, *Li Chi*, 2:313. "Do not roll the rice into a ball" passage is based on the translation in Legge, *Li Chi*, 1:80–81. "The instructive and transforming power of rituals" passage is based on Legge, *Li Chi*, 2:259–60. "In music the sages found pleasure" passage is based on the translation in Legge, *Li Chi*, 2:107. "A filial son, in nourishing his aged" passage is based on the translation in Legge, *Li Chi*, 1:467–68. "Although his parents be dead" passage is based on the translation in Legge, *Li Chi*, 1:457.

Chapter 3: Government in Confucian teachings

For oracle bone inscriptions, see W. T. de Bary, *Sources of Chinese Tradition*, 2nd ed., 2 vols. (New York: Columbia University Press, 1999), 1: 3–23. "Now, Zhou, the great king of Shang," from the *Book of History*, is based on James Legge's translation in *The Shoo King or Book of Historical Documents*, vol. 3, *The Chinese Classics*, 284–85. "Wailing and calling to heaven" passage is based on the translation in Legge, *The Shoo King*, 426. "Heaven sees as the people sees" passage is based on the translation in Legge, *The Shoo King*, 292. "The Mandate is not easy to keep" passage from the *Book of Odes* is translated in de Bary, *Sources of Chinese Tradition*, 1:39 (with slight modification here). "The empire is not an individual's private property" is cited in Frederic Wakeman Jr. *The Fall of Imperial China* (New York: Free Press, 1975), 81.

Chapter 4: Variety within early Confucianism

References to the *Mencius* text are to standard book, part, and passage number (e.g., 6A.2 is Book 6, Part A, passage 2); references to the *Xunzi* text are to standard section number. Translations of the *Mencius* are from Gardner, *The Four Books* or D. C. Lau, *Mencius* (Hammondsworth: Penguin, 1970), with occasional slight revision. Translations of the *Xunzi* are from Burton Watson, *Xunzi* (New York: Columbia University Press, 2003), with occasional slight revision.

Chapter 5: The reorientation of the Confucian tradition after 1000 CE: The teachings of Neo-Confucianism

"Be they adults or children" is from the *Conversations of Master Chu* [Zhu Xi's *Zhuzi yulei*], translated in Daniel K. Gardner, *Learning to Be a Sage* (Berkeley: University of California Press, 1990), 12. "Qi moves and flows in all directions" is based on the translation in de Bary, *Sources of Chinese Tradition*, 1:687. "Heaven is my father" is found in de Bary, *Sources of Chinese Tradition*, 1:683. "The interaction of the two *qi*" is based on the translation in W. T. Chan, *Source Book in Chinese Philosophy* (Princeton: Princeton University Press, 1963), 463. Zhu Xi's explanations of principle are cited in Gardner, *Learning to Be a Sage*, 90, with slight modification here. The discussion of Zhu Xi's understanding of human nature and the self-cultivation process is based on Gardner, *The Four Books*, 133–38. "Human nature is simply this principle" and "human nature is principle" passages are cited in Gardner, *Learning to Be a Sage*, 98, with slight revision here. "Those of antiquity" is translated in Gardner, *The Four Books,* 5. "What is meant by the extension of knowledge" passage is translated in Gardner, *The Four Books*, 8. Zhu Xi's remarks about letting go of the mind and preserving the mind are cited in Gardner, *Learning to Be a Sage*, 51. The summary of the program of learning is drawn from Gardner, introduction to *The Four Books* and Gardner, *Learning to Be a Sage*, 35–6. "All things in the world have principle" is cited in Gardner, *Learning to Be a Sage*, 63. "Ease, immediacy, and brevity" is Zhu's description of the Four Books, cited in Gardner, *Learning to Be a Sage*, 39. "In reading, begin with passages" is from Gardner, *Learning to Be a Sage*, 43–4. A translation of Zhu Xi's hermeneutics can be found in Gardner, *Learning to Be a Sage*, 128–62. "In reading, you want both body and mind" is found in Gardner, *Learning to Be a Sage*, 146. "When the number's sufficient" is from Gardner, *Learning to Be a*

Sage, 136. "Practice the Way with all his strength" is cited in Gardner, *Learning to Be a Sage*, 38.

Chapter 6: Confucianism in practice

John Chaffee, *Thorny Gates of Learning in Sung China* (Cambridge: Cambridge University Press, 1985), 15, estimates that successful candidates in the examination accounted for 6–16 percent of the pre-Song civil service. On cheating in the examinations, see Benjamin Elman, *A Cultural History of Civil Examinations in Late Imperial China* (Berkeley: University of California Press, 2000), 174–205; and Chung-li Chang, *The Chinese Gentry* (Seattle: University of Washington Press, 1955), 188–97. On Confucian critiques of the examination system, see David S. Nivison, "Protest Against Conventions and Conventions of Protest," in Arthur Wright, ed., *The Confucian Persuasion* (Stanford, CA: Stanford University Press, 1960), 177–201. For instances of uxorilocal marriage, where the husband moves in with the wife's family, see Susan Mann, *The Talented Women of the Zhang Family* (Berkeley: University of California Press, 2007). "Nothing is better" passage is from Ban Zhao's *Lessons for Women* and is found in Nancy Lee Swann, *Pan Chao, Foremost Woman Scholar of China, First Century A.D.* (New York: Century Co., 1932), with slight modification. Passages from the *Analects for Women* are from de Bary, *Sources of Chinese Tradition*, 1:830–31. Zeng Jifen's remark, "To whom, then, does the responsibility" is cited by Joseph McDermott, "The Chinese Domestic Bursar," *Ajia bunka kenkyū*, November 1990, 18–19.

Epilogue: Confucianism in the twentieth and twenty-first centuries

"Began to see the words between the lines" is from Hsien-yi Yang and Gladys Yang's translation, "A Madman's Diary," in *Selected Stories of Lu Hsun* [Lu Xun] (Peking: Foreign Language Press, 1972), 10. Chiang Kai-shek's "New Life Movement" speech of 1934 is translated in de Bary, *Sources of Chinese Tradition*, 2:342. The telegram, "Dearest Chairman Mao" is cited in Sang Ye and Geremie Barmé, "Commemorating Confucius in 1966–67," *China Heritage Quarterly*, no. 20 (December 2009) http://www.chinaheritagequarterly.org/scholarship.php?searchterm=020_confucius.inc&issue=020. The editorial in the *People's Daily* appeared on January 10, 1967.

Further reading

General studies of early Chinese intellectual history

Graham, A. C. *Disputers of the Tao: Philosophical Argumentation in Ancient China*. La Salle, IL: Open Court, 1989.

Schwartz, Benjamin I. *The World of Thought in Ancient China*. Cambridge, MA: Harvard University Press, 1985.

Van Norden, Bryan W. *Introduction to Classical Chinese Philosophy*. Indianapolis, IN: Hackett Publishing, 2011.

Translations of Confucian texts

A. The *Analects*

Brooks, E. Bruce, and Taeko Brooks. *The Original Analects: Sayings of Confucius and His Successors*. New York: Columbia University Press, 1998.

Lau, D. C. *The Analects/Confucius*. London: Penguin Books, 1979.

Slingerland, Edward. *Confucius Analects: With Selections from Traditional Commentaries*. Indianapolis, IN: Hackett Publishing, 2003.

Waley, Arthur. *The Analects of Confucius*. New York: Vintage, 1989.

B. The *Mencius*

Lau, D. C. *Mencius*. Hammondsworth: Penguin, 1970.

Van Norden, Bryan W. *Mengzi: With Selections from Traditional Commentaries*. Indianapolis, IN: Hackett Publishing, 2008.

C. The *Xunzi*

Knoblock, John. *Xunzi: A Translation and Study of the Complete Works*, 3 vols. Stanford, CA: Stanford University Press, 1988–94.

Watson, Burton. *Xunzi: Basic Writings*. New York: Columbia University Press, 2003.

D. The *Book of Rites*

Legge, James. *Li Chi: The Book of Rites*, 2 vols. New Hyde Park, NY: University Press, 1967.

E. The Four Books

Gardner, Daniel K. *The Four Books: The Basic Teachings of the Later Confucian Tradition*. Indianapolis, IN: Hackett Publishing, 2007.

Studies of early Confucian thought

Fingarette, Herbert. *Confucius: The Secular as Sacred*. New York: Harper & Row, 1972.

Goldin, Paul. *Rituals of the Way: The Philosophy of Xunzi*. Chicago: Open Court, 1999.

Ivanhoe, Philip J. *Confucian Moral Self-Cultivation*. Indianapolis, IN: Hackett Publishing, 2000.

Loewe, Michael. *Dong Zhongshu: A "Confucian" Heritage and the Chunqiu fanlu*. Leiden; Boston: Brill, 2011.

Makeham, John. *Transmitters and Creators: Chinese Commentators and Commentaries on the Analects*. Cambridge, MA: Harvard University Press, 2003.

Nylan, Michael. *The Five "Confucian" Classics*. New Haven, CT: Yale University Press, 2001.

Queen, Sarah. *From Chronicle to Canon: The Hermeneutics of the Spring and Autumn Annals, according to Tung Chung-shu*. Cambridge: Cambridge University Press, 1996.

Van Norden, Bryan W., ed. *Confucius and the Analects: New Essays*. Oxford: Oxford University Press, 2002.

Studies of later Confucian thought

de Bary, Wm. Theodore, ed. *Self and Society in Ming Thought*. New York: Columbia University Press, 1970.

de Bary, Wm. Theodore, ed. *The Unfolding of Neo-Confucianism*. New York: Columbia University Press, 1975.

Bol, Peter. *Neo-Confucianism in History*. Cambridge, MA: Harvard University Asia Center. Distributed by Harvard University Press, 2008.

Chow, Kai-wing. *The Rise of Confucian Ritualism in Late Imperial China: Ethics, Classics, and Lineage Discourse*. Stanford, CA: Stanford University Press, 1994.

Gardner, Daniel K. *Learning to Be a Sage: Selections from the Conversations of Master Chu, Arranged Topically*. Berkeley: University of California Press, 1990.

Graham, A. C. *Two Chinese Philosophers: Ch'eng Ming-tao and Ch'eng Yi-chuan*. London: Lund Humphries, 1958.

McMullen, David. *State and Scholars in T'ang China*. Cambridge: Cambridge University Press, 1988.

Tillman, Hoyt. *Confucian Discourse and Chu Hsi's Ascendancy*. Honolulu: University of Hawaii Press, 1992.

Tu, Wei-ming. *Neo-Confucian Thought in Action: Wang Yang-ming's Youth (1472–1509)*. Berkeley: University of California Press, 1976.

Wilson, Thomas. *Genealogy of the Way: The Construction and Uses of the Confucian Tradition in Late Imperial China*. Stanford, CA: Stanford University Press, 1995.

Wright, Arthur, ed. *The Confucian Persuasion*. Stanford, CA: Stanford University Press, 1960.

Education and the examination system

de Bary, Wm. Theodore, and John W. Chaffee, eds. *Neo-Confucian Education: The Formative Stage*. Berkeley: University of California Press, 1989.

Chafee, John W. *The Thorny Gates of Learning in Sung China: A Social History of Examinations*. Cambridge: Cambridge University Press, 1985.

Elman, Benjamin A. *A Cultural History of Civil Examinations in Late Imperial China*. Berkeley: University of California Press, 2000.

Elman, Benjamin A., and Alexander Woodside, eds. *Education and Society in Late Imperial China, 1600–1900*. Berkeley: University of California Press, 1994.

Miyazaki, Ichisada. *China's Examination Hell: The Civil Service Examinations of Imperial China*. New Haven, CT: Yale University Press, 1981.

Wu, Jingzi. *The Scholars*. Translated by Gladys Yang. Rockville, MD: Silk Pagoda, 2006.

Confucianism and the state

Chang, Chung-li. *The Chinese Gentry: Studies on Their Role in Nineteenth-Century Chinese Society*. Seattle: University of Washington Press, 1955.

Dardess, John. *Blood and History: The Donglin Faction and its Repression, 1620–27*. Honolulu: University of Hawaii Press, 2002.

Elliott, Mark C. *Emperor Qianlong: Son of Heaven, Man of the World*. New York: Longman, 2009.

Huang, Liu-hung. *A Complete Book Concerning Happiness and Benevolence: A Manual for Local Magistrates in Seventeenth Century China*. Tucson: University of Arizona Press, 1984.

Huang, Ray. *1587, A Year of No Significance: The Ming Dynasty in Decline*. New Haven, CT: Yale University Press, 1981.

Guy, R. Kent. *The Emperor's Four Treasuries: Scholars and State in the late Ch'ien-lung Era*. Cambridge, MA: Council on East Asian Studies, Harvard University. Distributed by Harvard University Press, 1987.

Confucianism and the family

Baker, Hugh. *Chinese Family and Kinship*. New York: Columbia University Press, 1979.

Cao, Xueqin. *The Story of the Stone: A Novel in Five Volumes*. Translated by David Hawkes. Hammondsworth: Penguin, 1973–86.

Ebrey, Patricia Buckley. *Chu Hsi's Family Rituals: A Twelfth-Century Manual for the Performance of Cappings, Weddings, Funerals, and Ancestral Rites*. Princeton, NJ: Princeton University Press, 1991.

Knapp, Ronald G., and Kai-yin Lo, eds. *House, Home, Family: Living and Being Chinese*. Honolulu: University of Hawaii Press, 2005.

Confucianism and women

Ebrey, Patricia Buckley. *The Inner Quarters: Marriage and the Lives of Women in the Sung Period*. Berkeley: University of California Press, 1993.

Ko, Dorothy. *Teachers of the Inner Chambers: Women and Culture in Seventeenth-Century China*. Stanford, CA: Stanford University Press, 1994.

Ko, Dorothy, Jahyun Kim Haboush, and Joan R. Piggot. *Women and Confucian Cultures in Premodern China, Korea, and Japan.* Berkeley: University of California Press, 2003.

Mann, Susan. *Precious Records: Women in China's Late Eighteenth Century.* Stanford, CA: Stanford University Press 1997.

Mann, Susan. *The Talented Women of the Zhang Family.* Berkeley: University of California Press, 2007.

Pruitt, Ida. *A Daughter of Han: The Autobiography of a Chinese Working Woman.* Stanford, CA: Stanford University Press, 1945.

Wang, Robin, ed. *Images of Women in Chinese Thought and Culture: Writings from the Pre-Qin Period through the Song Dynasty.* Indianapolis, IN: Hackett Publishing, 2003.

Confucianism since the twentieth century

Alitto, Guy. *The Last Confucian: Liang Shu-ming and the Chinese Dilemma of Democracy,* 2nd ed. Berkeley: University of California Press, 1986.

Chow, Tse-tsung. *The May Fourth Movement: Intellectual Revolution in Modern China.* Cambridge, MA: Harvard University Press, 1960.

Harrison, Henrietta. *The Man Awakened from Dreams: One Man's Life in a North China Village, 1875–1942.* Stanford, CA: Stanford University Press, 2005.

Levenson, Joseph R. *Confucian China and Its Modern Fate: A Trilogy.* Berkeley: University of California Press, 1968.

Lin, Yü-sheng. *The Crisis of Chinese Consciousness: Radical Antitraditionalism in the May Fourth Era.* Madison: University of Wisconsin Press, 1979.

Louie, Kam. *Critiques of Confucius in Contemporary China.* Hong Kong: The Chinese University Press, 1980.

Yu, Dan. *Confucius from the Heart: Ancient Wisdom for Today's World.* New York: Atria Books, 2009.

Index

A

Ai, Duke, 35
Analects, 3–4, 8, 11, 14–15
  East Asia, influence in, 8
  family, 30, 100
  government, 40–43
  heaven, 13–14, 45
  learning, 19–22, 80, 91
  Mandate of Heaven (*tianming*)
    and, 45
  modern-day applications of, 118,
    119
  morally superior man, 18, 22,
    25, 42
  opening passage of, 17*f*
  rectification of names, 57
  ritual (*li*), 13, 22, 25–26, 27–28
  ruler, 34, 39, 43
  true goodness (*ren*), 22–25, 42
  women, 104–5, 108 (see also
    Analects for Women)
  Xunzi, comparison with, 50
  Yu Dan on, 119
  Zhu Xi and, 80–82
Analects for Women, 108, 109, 110
ancestors
  Chinese culture, 97, 101–4
  importance in the family, 101,
    102*f*, 102–4
marriage, 106
ritual practice, 26, 27, 28, 102*f*,
  102–4
ancestral rites, 101–4, 102*f*
"Announcement to the Prince of
  Kang, The," 38

B

ba (hegemon, strongman). *See*
  hegemon
"backing the book," memorization,
  91, 91*f*
Ban Zhao, 105, 107, 108, 110
Beijing Normal University
  117, 119
Beijing Olympic Committee, 118
Beijing University, 114, 118, 119
Bible, 48, 81
Book of Changes, 4, 6, 81
Book of Filial Piety, 105, 108
Book of History, 4, 5, 6, 10, 13, 20,
  38, 44–47, 60, 81
Book of Odes, 4, 5, 6, 10, 13, 20, 29,
  38, 46–47
Book of Poetry, 60, 81, 105
Book of Rites, 4, 5, 6, 25, 26, 27, 28,
  30–31, 81, 101
Bo Yi, 11
Buddhism, 8, 71, 84, 104

C